A Place to Call Home

a memoir

by

Faye Schreder

Published by:
Greenetree Press
369 15th St N
Sartell, MN 56377
320-240-2996
greenetreepress@hotmail.com

ISBN: 0-9801680-0-7
ISBN 13: 978-0-9801680-0-6

Dedication

❧❦

Although this book is a gift to you, my grandchildren, it is dedicated to my own eleven children, your parents. The Schreder children are Debbie, Bonnie, Mike, Kevin, Scott, Pat, Jamie, Brian, Nancy, Mari, and Amy.

Your parents are wonderful, special people. They are kind, generous and giving, deserving of your utmost respect. You will never fully understand how much each of them, without exception, has contributed to our large family in extraordinary measure. I have a deep and abiding love for each of them, and I am eternally grateful to call them son or daughter.

I love all of you grandchildren as well, and I am proud of you. You each possess unique gifts, which bring a special dimension of joy to our family.

The stories in this book go back more than seventy years, but the small child on these pages is not so different from children of today. The memories contain joys, hopes, and struggles, much like you experience.

These little stories recall a simpler time and a more humble way of life. They are based on remembered family experiences during my childhood and provide a glimpse into the way things were in our family during the 1930s and '40s. I want to tell you how it was before those days are lost completely.

The story of family is a never-ending tale with unique memories for each of us. I challenge you, children and grandchildren, to pick up a pen and add your own recollections and reflections to the continuing saga.

Much Love,
Faye Schreder

Acknowledgements

ಬಿ೧೩

A special thank you to my parents, the late Ben and Lillian Bromenschenkel, who taught me the value of honesty, simplicity, and perseverance in the face of challenges. Thank you, also to my eleven brothers and sisters. I consider it a privilege to have grown up in our large family, and some of my best friends are family members. I appreciate the encouragement I receive in my writing from so many relatives.

A special thank you to Seal Dwyer. I will be forever grateful for the inspiration, expertise, encouragement and confidence she has given me in completing this project.

Contents

ഇരരു

Preface

My parents were married seven years, and I was their sixth child. They were married in November of 1929, a scant month after the onset of the Great Depression. This depression, a world-wide business slump, was considered the worst and longest period of unemployment in modern history.

Farm prices dropped in the early 1920s and remained so low that most farmers were unable to pay the mortgage on their farms. As a result, many banks in the farm areas were forced to go out of business. At the same time, industrial production increased, but wages did not, so workers had no money to buy the new products. There was less money in circulation, causing businesses to suffer. In 1929, America's entire economic system was on the verge of collapse. Then, stock values plunged, causing banks, factories, and stores to close. When the banks closed, the savings of millions of people were lost.

As if these factors didn't create enough hardship in our country in the 1930s, the problems were compounded by a drought through out most of our nation's midsection. With rainfall far below average and higher than normal temperatures, the crops withered and died, then the topsoil dried out, crumbled and blew away on hot, dry winds. The drought affected the entire nation, with food becoming scarce and prices high.

Unable to make a living on farms, people abandoned them in droves, searching for employment. But, there were no jobs available, and millions of people were out of work and penniless, with no alternative but to depend on the government or charity for food. Ours was a culture of people who had always worked hard and sacrificed to "take care of their own," and it was difficult for them to stand in bread lines to feed their hungry children.

This was the economic situation when my parents began their life together. During those depression years, they eked out a living by renting one of the many farms available because of foreclosures. We lived on farms known simply as "Jake's place" and "Matt's place," probably former owners. With a few head of dairy cattle, some chickens and pigs, and a few pieces of old horse-drawn farm implements, my parents were able to support their growing family.

The farm house, often in disrepair and with no telephone, electricity, plumbing, or central heat, would give the family a roof over our heads. The livestock would provide us with meat, milk, and eggs. Along with this, they planted huge gardens and preserved the food in Mason jars each summer for winter consumption. My father trapped and sold muskrat pelts in the winter to supplement the family income. If there were extra garden products, chickens, or eggs, these, too, were sold. We were poor, but it was very important for my parents to be self-supporting, and they didn't accept any kind of welfare or "dole," as my father called it.

MEMORIES

Images
tap gently
to get
my attention,
play
hide and seek
with
my memory.

Bring joy
like
ice crystals
exploding
in the sun,
wrap me
in a chrysalis
of colors.

Then fade
into the mist,
waft
through
my fingertips
without
a
backward
glance.

A New Baby

৩৩৫৩

Mama's sleep was interrupted by a dull surge of pain. She moaned softly, and dozed for another twenty minutes, until the next wave passed through her body, Then, breathing deeply, she pushed back the homemade patch-work quilt and eased her cumbersome form out of the warm bed.

The dark, still farmhouse was chilly as she groped her way through the living room and into the kitchen. Reaching for the match-box on the wall behind the stove, she lit the kerosene lamp. Its flame cast a soft glow over the oilcloth-covered table, but left the outer edges of the room in shadows. The fire had burned itself out in the kitchen stove, and the linoleum was cold on her bare feet.

On her way back to the bedroom, she

Ben and Lillian Bromenschenkel, ca 1935.

stopped at the space heater in the living room to stoke the fire. The embers crackled and sparks flew as she stirred the coals with the poker and added another chunk of wood. A pretty, energetic woman, with short black hair framing a youthful face, she was sober and pensive in the early morning stillness. Before closing the stove door, she stood close to the flames for a few moments, absorbing their warmth and contemplating the task that lay ahead.

In the shadowy, unlit bedroom, she dressed quietly, pausing only when a wave of pain flowed through her lower back and pelvis. The only sounds were her labored breathing and the crackling fire in the adjacent room. Her largest housedress fit snugly as she pulled it over her hard, protruding belly. Sitting on the edge of the bed, she struggled to reach her feet as she pulled on brown, cotton stockings, fastening

Jean (back), Dennis, Faye, and Bernice Bromenschenkel, 1937.

them above her knees with round elastic garters. Finally, she slipped her swollen feet into a pair of worn, leather oxfords. She needed new shoes, but now

Our family. (Back) Carol, Bernice, Jerry,Dick, Dennis, Faye. (Front) Kenny, Mary Ann, Ben, Lillian holding Connie, Jean Bernie, Walt. 1950.

with six small children in the house and Christmas coming, the shoes would have to wait. Straining once again, she reached for the shoelaces and tied them loosely.

It was 3:00 a.m. when Mama reached behind her and nudged Daddy awake. "It's time to leave for the hospital, Ben," she murmured. Instantly wide-awake and into his clothes, he tapped on his youngest sister Loretta's door, to tell her that he and Mama were leaving. He spoke softly so as not to awaken the five small children sleeping nearby. In the morning, Loretta will get them up, dress them and cook oatmeal for their breakfast. She will stay in the house to take care of the children during Mama's absence, and as long as she's needed after her return. When she's finished here, she will likely move on to the home of another family member. Having neither a marriage nor a career, she is expected to "help out" at the homes of her siblings at times such as this.

In the kitchen, Mama slipped into her winter coat, draped a scarf over her head and tied it under her chin like a babushka, while Daddy kindled a fire in the cookstove. The aroma of yesterday's baking still lingered as she glanced at

Dennis and Faye Bromenschenkel, 1938.

the freshly baked pastry on the counter of her small cupboard. Her thoughts returned to the morning before, when she baked the holiday bread. Then, she and Loretta carved pumpkins, cooked them and made them into pies. Later, Daddy went to the henhouse, caught two chickens, beheaded them on the chopping block and butchered them for Thanksgiving. Today, since she wouldn't be home, Loretta would cook and serve the holiday meal for Daddy and the children.

Daddy shrugged into his coat, cap and mittens and Mama blew out the flame in the lamp. They softly pulled the kitchen door shut behind them and stepped out into the frosty darkness. It was a starry, clear night as Daddy, anxious to be on the way, hurried to start the car while his usually petite wife walked heavily across the light snow in the farmyard, carrying her small suitcase. He inserted the crank into the front of the 1927 Chevrolet; after two or three swift turns, the engine ignited and he breathed a sigh of relief. He helped Mama into the cold car, scraped the frost from the windows with his mittened hand, and they began the thirteen-mile drive over deserted gravel roads to the St. Cloud hospital.

Jerry and Dennis, 1938.

At 10:00 a.m. on Thursday, November 26, their daughter was born to thirty-eight year-old Ben and twenty-five year-old Lillian Carlin Bromenschenkel. After a hospital stay of eight days, Mama brought the brown-eyed, dark haired baby to the small farm they rented near St. Wendell, MN

A few short days later, on December 6, the baby was brought to St. Columbkill's Catholic Church to be christened.

Jerry and Dennis with a little sister, 1938.

Jean, Faye, and Bernice Bromenschenkel, 1938.

According to the church, the sacrament of Baptism was essential to become a child of God, eligible to enter the kingdom of Heaven. Therefore, the rite must be performed at the first opportunity. Parents would take no chances on an infant succumbing to an illness, unbaptized, and spend eternity in Limbo. The baby was dressed in a white gown, a symbol of purity. The holy water poured over her head would wash original sin from her soul, make her a child of God, and give her a name as well. When Mama wanted to name the baby 'Faye Ellen,' the priest objected. "That's not a saint's name," he said. "You must name her 'Frances,' but you may call her 'Faye.'"

Thus began my life in the family and the church. My companions on our journey through childhood were my eleven brothers and sisters. They are: Jean, Dick, Bernice, Jerry, Dennis, Carol, Ken, Mary Ann, Walt, Bernie, and Connie. Each has added a unique perspective and a distinct set of memories to my life.

The Yellow Brick House

❦

Our family moved three times during my first five years, always renting a small farm in central Minnesota. From St. Wendell, we moved to "Jake Neuman's Place," then to the last farm we rented about 1940, "Matt Voerding's Place," near Duelm in Benton County.

This farmsite still stands on a little knoll on the corner of Highway 95 and 95th Avenue Northeast. It is marked by a huge pine tree, still a visible landmark, which rises from a corner of the yard and towers above the buildings and trees like a sentinel.

I loved the two-story, yellow brick farmhouse with the gabled attic and the open porch which stretched along the

Carol, Kenny, and Faye by yellow brick house. 1940.

entire front side. Facing the southern sun, it served as a play-room for us most of the year. In the fall, our playmates and older siblings went off down the road to the country school. Then, Carol, three-year old Kenny, and I had the porch to ourselves, as well as the wooden swing which hung by a rope from the branch of an elm tree near the house.

Inside, in the large dining room, stood a round oak table, used mostly for playing school. When they came home from school in the afternoon, our older siblings gathered us around the table and taught us to count, say the ABCs and write our names. We practiced our small motor skills by learning to tie our shoes and cutting pictures from old Sears and Roebuck catalogs.

Mama was a wonderful storyteller with a vast repertoire of fairy tales and Mother Goose rhymes, which she taught us while rocking the babies, washing dishes, and especially while sewing or ironing our clothes. We children, in turn, were called upon to entertain our younger siblings in the same manner. If Mama was busy, and a little one fussing, she'd instruct, "tell a story," and a six-year-old would distract the toddler with tales of Peter Rabbit or the Three Billy Goats Gruff.

On a cold afternoon in December of 1941, friends of my parents drove up the driveway, parked their car and knocked on the kitchen door. In a somber manner, they greet-ed Mama and Daddy. "The Japanese have bombed Pearl Harbor!" they announced. That night at the suppertable, the adults' conversation harkened to the days of World War I, when my father was in the army. They spoke of friends they had lost and expressed fears of another carnage. We children were subdued, sensing the gravity of the situation.

During the late '30s and early '40s, the country was still feeling the effects of the Great Depression, as well as the drought of the dust-bowl years. Many people had little money and were in need of a home. For a short time during our stay in the yellow house, the parlor, which extended across the entire front of the house, was closed off and occupied by a hapless young couple who needed a home. Although it was forbidden, sometimes, when Carol and I were sent upstairs for an afternoon nap, we'd slide open the heat register on the floor and spy through the grates at our downstairs neighbors, hoping to get a glimpse of the fat baby who lived with his parents in the parlor below.

Meanwhile, the farm owner, retired and alone, also occupied an upstairs bedroom. So, for part of the year that our large family lived in the house, two other families had also taken up residence there.

Our upstairs resident kept mostly to himself. He seldom left his room in the daytime, but sometimes thumped on the floor with his cane if our family became too noisy. Each day he received two eggs and a pint of milk from us, which were taken to his door.

Since we seldom saw him, Carol and I thought of him as a ghost in the house and were afraid of him. One day, Mama handed us the milk and eggs; she told us to take them upstairs and knock on his door. As we stood at the foot of the stairs, it seemed like a long, scary way to the top. We walked slowly, our elbows touching. When we finally reached his door at the top of the stairs and knocked timidly, the door opened slowly and an unsmiling, white-haired man appeared. He solemnly and silently reached for the jar of milk from Carol, then extended his other hand, and one at a time, I dropped the eggs into it.

"Wait here," he said and disappeared for a moment. We were too frightened to run, so did as we were told. When he came back, he leaned down and said, "Whisper in my ear what you would like."

Startled, but with presence of mind, we each whispered, "Candy!" Whereupon, he opened our palms and dropped three little mints into each. Then, his face wrinkling into a shy smile, he turned and silently closed the door. We walked back downstairs slowly, savoring the minty softness on our tongues. That day the ghost in our house became a real person, and we were no longer afraid of him.

COUNTRY CHURCH

She picks absently
at a scab on her knee,
scratches her elbow,
chews the end
of her braid.

Squirming between
silent, humid parents
on the sticky bench,
skinny legs
dangle.

Silence explodes
like tiny rockets.
Her body tingles
with desire
to escape
droning prayers.

A fly,
confused
by choices
flits from
flowery cologne
to sticky spray
on salt and pepper
hair.

She flicks it
from her face,
watches wistfully
as it escapes
through
an open window.

St. Lawrence Church

୫୬ୠ୦ୡ

Around the turn of the century, a church sprang up on the horizon every few miles across the rural central Minnesota landscape. It was common for ethnic and religious groups arriving in the United States in the late nineteenth century, to settle with their own kind in a given area. A school and a church would be the first structure to be built in the community, with a country store next on the scene. With card parties, church suppers and bazaars, as well as the celebration of all the sacraments, the church served not only as a place of

Faye and Dennis Bromenschenkel, 1941.

Katherine and Robert Carlin. Jean, Dennis, Dick, and Faye Bromenschenkel, 1941.

worship, but as a social outlet for the rural populace. Usually surrounded by oak, maple, or elm trees, with a generous sprinkling of pines, its steeple quickly became a landmark in the community, and the peal of church bells resonated across prairies and woods.

Bernice, Carol, Kenny, and Faye,1941.

Each Sunday, our family, with shoes polished and dressed in our best clothing, attended such a church. When we lived in the yellow brick house, we belonged to St. Lawrence Catholic Church in Duelm.

The backyard of the church served as a final resting place for generations of faithful, their souls in heaven and physical presence obscured by a blanket of sod. A carved stone at the head of each grave served to commemorate their existence as well as to remind us all of our ultimate destiny.

In this church, the two eldest children in our family, Jean and Dick, made their solemn communion. Jean wore a beautiful white dress and veil, and Dick was resplendent in a white shirt, necktie, and blue sport jacket.

It was the custom for preschoolers, two boys and two girls, to act as Angels to accompany each communicant from their pew to the altar railing to receive the Eucharist. My brother Dennis and I were chosen to be two of the Angels. We had to practice before the big day, and I remember walking down the dusty country road to church. Dennis and I, too, must be dressed all in white, so it was a big responsibility for Mama to dress four of her children for this special occasion. She sat at her treadle sewing machine late into the night and did us up in fine style as she did in so many ways because of the love and pride she had for her children.

Once a year, in spring, we celebrated the feast of Corpus Christe, or Body of Christ, with a procession through the cemetery after Mass. Early on Corpus Christe morning, Mama took the time to help us pick fragrant lilacs and lilies of the valley, wild honeysuckle and daisies, then put the petals into small baskets to be distributed during the procession.

After the final blessing at Mass, the priest and Mass servers led a procession through the cemetery. Directly behind them, a six-foot cross bearing the image of Jesus was carried by a parishioner. Then came the children with baskets of flower petals to be strewn along the way. The adults and babies made up the rest of the procession.

At age four and five, this was the first year for Carol and me to walk with the big children. It was a beautiful spring morning with sun shining on our faces and bare arms. We felt light and free as we carried our flower petals along the emerald green paths, with birds singing as a background to the litany of prayers recited along the way.

In the older section of the cemetery, there was a small gray tombstone that caught my eye. It's surface was discolored and chipped, the words barely legible. A lamb carved from stone rested upon its top. I hesitated for a moment, and an older girl poked me with her elbow, telling me to keep moving. "What does it say on this stone?" I asked her.

"It's a baby's grave," she answered. "A little girl, born May 11, and died May 12. That means she was one day old."

"One day old! Her mother hardly had a chance to hold her!" I exclaimed. The tiny baby lingered in my mind as we wound through rows of gravestones. I imagined the baby's mother leaving pink wild rose blossoms at her grave, their fragile petals falling to the grass and mingling with her tears.

When the procession ended and people sauntered away, I glanced at my basket. It still contained the wilting flower petals that I had forgotten to strew. Quickly, I darted back to the lamb tombstone and scattered the fragrant petals on the baby's grave, then joined my family at the car for the ride home.

A Place of Our Own

⍵⍵⍺⍺

During my fifth year, my parents bought an eighty-acre tract of land from Grandfather Jacob Bromenschenkel. It was located along County Road 47, four miles east of St. Cloud.

On a beautiful late spring day Carol, Dennis and I rode into St. Cloud with Mama and Daddy on a shopping trip. On the way home, Daddy parked our Model A Ford alongside a gravel road next to a hay field. He stepped down into the three-foot ditch and up the other side. We stayed in the car with Mama and gazed across the flat, treeless, eighty-acre

Carol, Mary Ann, Walt, and Faye, 1944.

Walt and Bernie, 1945.

plot, while Daddy tramped through the knee-high clover blossoms, surveying the acreage. Mama explained to us that this is where we would soon be living. She pointed out where we would put our house. "The barn will go over there, she said, and the granary near the barn." Then she added, "We'll have to live in the granary until we get the house built."

We could see Grandpa Bromenschenkel's farm across the field just a half-mile away. A widower, he lived there with his son, Hank, and his family. They had only one child, Agnes, who would be in the first grade in the fall, like me. Down the road a quarter mile, we could see the white one-room District Sixty schoolhouse that sat at the corner of Daddy's field. His brother, Leo and his family were neighbors, too. Their son, Ray, would also be my classmate, coming to school with three older siblings. Two miles away, around the bend in the road, Aunt Marie and Uncle Ed Prom lived with their eight children. Of the twenty-five students attending school in grades one through eight that year, over half would be my brothers and sisters or cousins.

Back in the big house, at suppertime that evening, as he sat around the kitchen table with Mama and their ten children, Daddy said, "We'll start building tomorrow."

Mary Ann, Kenny, and Walt, 1943.

We children begged to tag along with the adults to the building site and many days we were allowed to accompany them. The aroma of fresh-cut lumber would forever remind us of the days when we played in the sun among the stacks of boards and partially constructed buildings at the site of our future home. We played hide and seek and tag around the board piles; and in the cool shelter of the doorless and windowless buildings, we played house, our carpet, the green grass of summer.

Summer flew quickly by. Clover blossoms turned brown, their stems trampled flat as the clover field was transformed into a farmyard. Time ground into eternity all too soon, as our parents struggled to provide shelter for the family and the animals before winter dropped its icy curtain upon us. First, the granary sprang up, then the barn and the chicken coop; a six-foot hole was dug by hand before an outhouse could be built. There seemed to be no end to the tasks before them. A well had to be drilled, fences erected, a driveway built across the steep ditch, and a mailbox installed. That first summer, there was little time to erect more than a basic shell for each building.

The buildings were erected on a treeless field, and as yet, there was neither time nor money to spend on trees. Those first years, our farmstead sweltered in the summer heat with no trees to gather the sky in its boughs and cool us under the shade of their branches. In winter, we were at the mercy of icy blasts from the northwest wind, as it swooped upon us with no windbreak to hold it at bay.

The granary, hardly bigger than a double garage, ceilingless, but partitioned by a seven-foot wall in the center, was used for our house. The front half would be our kitchen and living area. The back room became the sleeping space. As soon as it consisted of four walls, windows, a door and a chimney, we loaded our meager possessions onto hayracks and said goodbye to the big yellow house. We hitched the racks to the car and pulled them eight miles over country roads, and then we moved in. From that point onward, it became our home and was never referred to as a granary again.

Into the kitchen, we brought our wood-burning cook stove, a small cupboard for dishes and food, a dresser for storing clothes, and the kitchen sink. The sink was made of porce-

Walt, Kenny, Bernie, and Mary Ann, 1949.

Dennis, Jerry, and Dick on the steps of the Minnesota State Capitol, 1942.

lain, a two by three foot rectangle with a drain hole. Encased in a homemade wooden stand, a ledge on the side held the pail of drinking water. We drank our water from a dipper—a small enamel container holding about a pint—looking like a long-handled saucepan, which stayed in the water pail all the time. When one wanted a drink of water, we simply dipped out what we needed and all drank from the same dipper.

The red and white enamel "wash dish" always sat in the sink. To wash our hands and face, we filled it from the water pail. Under the sink, there was space for a five-gallon pail, which caught the used water. Potato peelings and leftover cooking scraps sometimes went into the pail, too; and each evening, the "slop pail" was carried out and emptied into the pigs' trough.

The Maytag wringer washing machine with a gas engine stood in one corner of the kitchen, to be pulled into the middle of the room on washday. Our round oak table, hand-me-down chairs, and homemade benches completed the furnishings. In late fall, a wood and coal-burning space heater was squeezed into the small kitchen to augment the heat from the cook stove.

In the second room, wires were strung from wall to wall with sheets over them, dividing the room into four tiny compartments barely big enough for a double bed in each. The only other piece of furniture was another dresser for storage space. We slept three to a double bed.

The first winter in this house was a difficult one. With no insulation or inner walls, and no ceiling in the two-room house, the floors were cold; and heat from our two stoves ascended straight to the peak, warming the rafters instead of us. Mama always kept her flat irons on the back of the stove where they stayed warm. At night, she wrapped them in a towel and slipped them under the quilts to keep our feet warm in bed. If the fires burned low overnight, our drinking water would be frozen in the pail when we awoke in the morning. Starting over in this primitive home was not easy, to be sure, but our parents would no longer be moving from farm to farm. At last, we had a place of our own.

School Days

Yesterday, Mama promised, "Tomorrow, you will start first grade!" Kindergarten was not offered in rural schools in the 1940s, so this would be my very first day of school, and I could hardly contain my excitement!

When I awoke, my older sister, Bernice, pulled open the bottom drawer of the dresser that stood in the kitchen. There, spread on top of the folded clothes, lay a beautiful, yellow organdy dress. I felt like a princess as I slipped it over my petticoat and turned around so Bernice could tie the sash in back. Then, I pulled on a pair of socks and my stiff new shoes. After Mama combed my hair, I was ready for my first day of school!

Interior of one-room school.

Country school similar to District 60. (Photo courtesy Stearns History Museum.)

It was a golden September morning in 1942, when my brother Dennis and I ran hand in hand down the field path to our little schoolhouse. The sun was shining into our faces as we ran. Ahead of us, a flock of blackbirds swooped into the ripening corn, and in the distance, we could hear the squawk of a pheasant as it skimmed the horizon.

We slowed down, and our hearts skipped a beat when we reached the school and climbed the broad concrete steps. The door was open, and we could see the teacher sitting at her desk as we entered the white frame building for the first time. The first students to arrive, we shyly introduced ourselves to a

[Back row] Gerald Bromenschenkel, Gerald Kowitz, cousin Theresa, Bernice Bromenschenkel, Darlene Busse. [Second row] Faye, cousins Ray and Clarence, Hilde Prom, Dennis Bromenschenkel. [Third row] Jerome Rosa, cousin Leo, Tom Gans, Maxine Busse, Carol Bromenschenkel, cousin Agnes. [Fourth row] cousin Jim, Allan Skoog, Lucille Prom, Ken Neeser, Alfred Prom. [Front row] Mary Ann Bromenschenkel, Jack Prom, DeWayne Eberhart, Roy Busse, Ken Bromenschenkel.

plumpish, soft-spoken woman whom we simply called "Teacher." This schoolroom, and the teacher we met that day, would be our sole source of formal education for the next six years.

The classroom was plain, with four or five huge curtainless windows on each side, providing the only source of light. The room still carried the closed-up, musty odor of books, chalk and sweeping compound. Now, with the entrance door open for the first time in months, these smells mingled with the late summer aroma of dry grass that wafted in, along with the sound of killdeer calling from the weeds along the edge of the schoolyard.

The teacher directed our attention to the tiny desks on the right hand side of the room reserved for first and second graders. We chose a desk and carefully placed our pencil into the slot at the top and laid our brand new five-cent tablet and box of eight crayons beside it. Then we went outdoors to play until the other students arrived and the school day began.

At nine o'clock, Teacher came out and rang the small brass bell that sat on her desk. We entered a classroom that was unembellished except for pictures of George Washington and Franklin Roosevelt, and a small American flag that hung from a bracket behind the teacher's desk. Above the blackboard, in front of the room hung a roll of maps, where each could be pulled down like a window shade to study the various countries. The only other adornment was the alphabet, which bordered the top of the blackboard across the front of the room.

The desks, carved with the initials of bygone students, were fastened together, one behind the other, in rows. They ranged in size from small to large, accommodating the twenty-five or thirty children in all eight grades. The bigger desks had hinges at the top that had to be lifted to put books inside.

Once we were settled in the classroom, we were not allowed to talk to each other during school time, but I didn't

[Top row] Hilde Prom, Faye, Maxine Busse, Carol Bromenschenkel, Lucille Prom, cousin Agnes. [Middle row] Dennis Bromenschenkel [Bottom row] Jack Prom, Mary Ann Bromenschenkel, Darlene Busse, DeWayne Eberhart, Jerome Rosa, Ken Neeser, Tom Gans, Allan Skoog, Alfred Prom, 1945.

mind because there were so many interesting things going on. The teacher gave the first-graders a book with a picture of a monkey on the cover. "You will be reading this," she said. "Take good care of it." I thought this was the most important moment of my life, the first book I ever had! I paged through it until she called the first grade to the front of the room. "The name of this book is Winky," she said. Then she read the first page, "Run, Winky, run!" When I went back to my seat, I read the words over and over. Learning to read was the beginning of such a joyful discovery, I knew my life would never be the same again. Newspapers, books, magazines, billboards and cereal boxes would now take on a new meaning.

Later, when everyone was studying, it was so quiet in the room that I could hear the ticking of the clock, as well as the songs of the red-winged blackbirds that perched on cattails in the pond across the road. I listened to these sounds while I was in school, reading!

As the year progressed, we settled into a routine that was simple but effective. With eight grades in one room, each

Lunch pails in a country school entryway.

class consisted of three or four students. In her quest to extricate weeds of illiteracy and plant seeds of curiosity, Teacher would call each grade to the front of the room while the rest of us were expected to study quietly at our desks. We had no audio or visual aids besides our books and blackboard, and much of what we learned was by a process of assimilation as we listened to the discussions of the teacher and .children of other grades.

With no electricity or indoor plumbing facilities, the students took turns each day carrying in a pail of fresh water from the pump outside the schoolhouse door. This provided us with our drinking water and was also used to fill the basin in which we washed our hands.

A huge wood and coal-burning stove stood in the front of the room, in which the teacher made a fire each morning, beginning in late Fall. The ceiling was high, and on bitterly cold days, the rising heat often left the floor cold and drafty so that we had to wear our boots and coats for the first few hours. Sometimes we would play a fast moving game of "Fruit basket upset" to warm up before we began studying.

Our bathroom facilities consisted of two outdoor toilets behind the schoolhouse and beyond the softball diamond. On winter days, a trip 'out back' proved to be a cold, difficult trek for little children. In lazy, Indian summer weather, though, or on balmy spring days, it was sometimes used as an excuse for a respite from tedious study, and one dawdled outdoors as long as possible. Often, on a solitary trip to the toilet, one could see a wild rabbit, a toad or a frog hopping across the quiet schoolyard. It was even more common to see the small green and yellow garter snakes slithering through the sandburs and dry grass. Although they were harmless, we small children were afraid of them. We soon learned to use the outhouse only during recess, when our friends or an older student could accompany us.

There were no indoor recreational opportunities, and our outdoor facilities and equipment were limited. There was a softball diamond for the older students with one bat and one softball. The rest of the students shared three swings, a slide and a set of 'chinning' bars. In warm weather, we also played games and jumped ropes that we brought from home. Our teacher seldom ventured outside as we played in the sandy, treeless yard. With no playground supervision and the lack of adequate equipment, our recesses often erupted in conflict and did not always depict the pastoral scene one would equate with a peaceful country schoolhouse.

Some of the girls played softball, and I tried it a few times. We didn't have baseball mitts, and one day when I was a fielder, I tried to catch a fly ball. The force sprained my finger, making it swollen and painful. After that, I waited until the ball was rolling to go after it, so I never knew the thrill of putting someone out. From then on, when the captains chose sides, they usually had enough players before they got to me.

The first three children out the door at recess usually got the swings. As an alternative, my little girlfriends and I migrated to the unused chinning bars. We wanted to swing by our knees, but since we all wore dresses to school, modesty prevented us from engaging in this activity. Even though most of our schoolmates were brothers and sisters or cousins, we were afraid the boys would tease us.

One day, first grader Maxine, came to school wearing a new pair of panties under her dress. She said that her parents told her to go ahead and play on the bars! With that announcement, she bravely climbed the lowest bar, hooked her legs over it and swung by her knees. Her skirt flapped over her head and dangling arms, exposing a bare tummy and new panties. She was our heroine of the day! All we needed was one brave soul to blaze the trail and rest of us soon followed suit.

The following year, when I began second grade, our teacher, Mrs. Schultz, distributed beautiful reading books to my classmates, Dennis, Ray, and Agnes. "Faye," she said. "I have a surprise for you," as she put a third-grade reader on my desk. "From now on you'll be in the third grade." My classmates were cousins Hilde Prom and Clarence Bromenschenkel. I was still only six years old and wouldn't be seven until the end of November. Second grade was exciting to me, and I didn't want to be a third grader. It wasn't long, though, before Hilde and I became fast friends, a bond we shared through high school and beyond.

School days quickly melted one into another, and soon I was in the fifth grade. I loved learning, but try as I might, I couldn't relate to fifth grade geography. Dull and boring diagrams and maps interspersed with dry text on the pages of my geography book left me confused and frustrated. I was still only eight years old and had no understanding of our countries regions, wheat belts, and corn belts. I couldn't relate to a nation's belt when the only ones I was familiar with were the one that held up Daddy's Sunday pants, or the one I had so much trouble tying on the back of my dress. Latitude and longitude, and river basins were equally confusing. To me, a basin was the one in the back of the classroom where we washed our hands after coming in from out back.

To explain concepts, Teacher rolled down the map of the United States, took her three-foot-long wand and quickly pointed to the areas in question, then rolled up the map, leaving me as confused as ever.

That one-room schoolhouse is gone now, and a housing development has taken its place. It was a way of life that had its disadvantages, but it gave the student a good education for the amount of money spent. Perhaps, somewhere between the frugal but intimate relationship between student and teacher of yesterday, and the more expansive but impersonal style of today, we could find an educational medium. We could offer our children the joy and value of a solid foundation in basic skills.

Grandma Carlin

༄༅

Pictures of my grandmother on her wedding day reveal the face of a lovely young woman. Her wide brimmed hat, bedecked with flowers and ribbon, crowned her head above thick, brown hair swept high from her forehead in a fashionable pompadour. The style, so popular at the turn of the century, emphasized her expressive brown eyes and serene countenance.

Katherine Dietrich, 1906.

I never knew my grandmother when she was that lovely young woman in the picture. By the time I came to know her, she was nearing seventy, and her beauty had stolen inward. She had a cheerful, kind, and gentle spirit, and embraced each of her grandchildren with an overflowing heart. My mother's children were her only grandchildren, and our hearts swelled with love for her, which she returned in full measure, enveloping all of us in the joyful glow of her tender affection.

Katherine Dietrich, the only grandmother we knew, was born on January 17, 1870, of immigrant parents. Her father was raised in the Catholic faith in France, and her mother came from a devout Lutheran family in Switzerland. The couple settled the issue of their interfaith marriage by raising their daughters in the Catholic faith, and their sons as Lutherans. Although she was Lutheran, Katherine's mother often hosted Father Pierz, a Catholic missionary, on his travels. He would offer mass for the sparse gathering of pioneers, using their kitchen table as an altar, when he passed through the Gilman area. The family harmoniously blended their traditions, culture, and religious practices, enabling Kathryn and her eight siblings to thrive in a close family relationship throughout their lives.

Katherine, or Kate as she was called, grew up on a dairy farm along the Elk River in Benton County, where fish were a staple in their diet. When Katherine was a little girl, the stable caught fire, and Kate's favorite mule perished in the blaze. The unfortunate event provided my soft-hearted grandmother with a sad childhood memory. When she was about ten years old, the family began farming near Clear Lake, Minnesota, always using horses and mules for power. She helped her mother with the many tasks required of women on a pioneer settlement until shortly before her marriage. Along with the endless household tasks, they made thick, round, cheeses, fourteen inches across, a tradition her mother brought from Switzerland.

Robert Carlin, 1906.

35

At age thirty-five, Katherine was still living at home with her parents when her father died. After his death, she moved into the village of Clear Lake with her mother and two brothers. As a child, her youngest brother Edward came down with measles and developed complications, resulting in mental retardation. Her older brother, Joseph, remained with his mother and brother, and worked as a handyman while caring for his aging mother until she passed away. Then, he continued to look after the disabled Edward, the two of them growing old together.

Katherine Dietrich, Robert Carlin wedding, June 9, 1907. Margaret Leary and Joseph Dietrich [back row].

In Clear Lake, Katherine met and married my grandfather, Robert Carlin, the son of Irish immigrants. She was thirty-seven and he was forty years old. Although the couple was nearing middle age at the time of their marriage, they became the parents of four children. Joseph Carlin was the oldest; and the second child, Lillian Rose, was my mother. The two younger siblings, Charlotte and Julia, died in infancy.

Robert and Katherine settled on a farm near Clear Lake. Less than four years after their marriage, when my mother was born, Kathryn was already forty-one years old, and a hard-working farm wife with a two-year-old son. Along with her housework, she could be found in the barn at chore time, feeding the animals she loved. She would also separate the milk from the cream in the little room off the kitchen. She would save the cream to make homemade butter, then take the skim milk back to the barn and feed it to the calves and pigs, finally performing the tedious task of washing the numerous disks of the separator.

As with all families, they were faced with sorrows, financial setbacks, and health problems during their lives, but they persevered in good humor on the farm, well into old age. They built a big, white house and barn on a picturesque farmstead, shaded with oak and birch trees, where horses whinnied and cattle grazed in the pasture. Although she had little money, it is said that Grandma was known widely for her charity and generosity. Grandpa and Grandma experienced the joy of raising two healthy children, as well as the inexplicable sadness of burying their last two babies, both within the first weeks of their lives.

On their infrequent shopping trips to St. Cloud, Grandpa and Grandma Carlin would stop by our small farm

Robert Carlin home, 1925.

Robert Carlin barn, 1925.

on their way home. Grandpa, always very straight of stature, businesslike and impersonal. Grandma, like a humble little wren in her brown dress, dark shoes, cotton stockings, and Sunday hat. She would sit on a straight wooden chair in our kitchen, and we children would be drawn to her like bees around a flower, vying for her attention. She praised us for helping Mama, for growing big, and for learning our prayers. "Our prayers are like a garden of flowers in Heaven," she would tell us. "Each time we pray, another flower is added to our heavenly garden." She was proud of us, and every now and then, a penny or a nickel would escape from her worn purse and appear in a delighted child's hand. The days were very special when we drove to the farm near Clear Lake to visit our grandparents in their big white house. We'd peek into the treasures of her attic storeroom, or play games in the guest room at the top of the stairs, sitting cross-legged on the huge oval rug that covered the chilly wooden floorboards. She had painstakingly braided it on cold winter days, or in the evenings when the chores were finished.

In the living room, we were fascinated by the writing desks and bookcases along the walls, filled with important

Robert Carlin, 1940.

looking books. One was a book of nostalgic poetry about Minnesota, written by Grandpa's uncle, Joseph Brady, who was a judge in California. Their precious items were protected by rounded glass on the doors, as were the huge oval engagement portraits of Grandpa and Grandma, looking down at us from where they hung, close to the ceiling. I loved to stand in the living room and look at the picture of the beautiful young woman with the gentle smile. Grandpa's face and hers were handsome and young, but old-fashioned to our childish eyes, and barely resembled our grandparents as we knew them.

We liked Grandma's kitchen the best, with its built-in cabinet connecting the kitchen and dining room. On the kitchen side, wooden doors concealed her everyday dishes. On the middle of her round, oak kitchen table stood an ornate, red and gold drinking glass from Switzerland. It held her silver teaspoons for stirring the coffee that brewed morning and evening in the enamel flecked coffee pot always on the kitchen stove.

The dining room side of the cabinet held Grandma's favorite possessions. This is where she kept the colorful dishes and serving bowls that her mother brought from Switzerland. They twinkled behind the glass doors when the morning sun shone through the dining room window.

On visits to their big farmhouse, while Grandpa sat aloofly in his captain's chair in the dining room, Grandma herded us into her kitchen, and found special treats in her cupboard for us. When we were outside with Grandpa, though, he would call us to the barn and show us his brightly colored Indian corn. We delighted in the colorful ears, and he would give us one to take home. Although he didn't often carry on a conversation with us, he was always kind.

One beautiful Sunday afternoon in the summer, when I was six, Grandma gathered us around her dining room table for cookies. Mama had sent seven-year-old Dennis out-

Katherine and Robert Carlin, 1941.

doors for a time-out because of a minor infraction, and it looked like he would miss the party!

"Let him come in," Grandma gently urged Mama.

"No," Mama stubbornly answered.

In her soft voice, Grandma repeatedly implored, "Just this once, let him come in." I stood with baited breath, fathoming the enormity of my brother's disappointment in missing out on Grandma's cookies. In her calm, unhurried manner, while putting cookies on a plate and filling drinking glasses from her milk pitcher, she continued to plead quietly for Dennis.

Finally, Mama relented. "You can call him in, Faye," she said.

Instantly, I flew through the kitchen, out onto the porch and down the steps, the screen door banging behind me. Dennis was standing dejectedly against the house.

"It's OK, you can come in!" I shouted. His face lit up, and we both raced back inside. We ate Grandma's cookies, drank her milk, and basked in the light of her love.

A year later, on August 27, 1943, our grandmother, at age seventy-three, quietly left this world and entered her flower garden in Heaven. This beautiful woman bequeathed a precious legacy to her grandchildren: the spirit of her undying affection.

A Steer in School

❧❧

Since we lived so close to the schoolhouse, our family always ran home for lunch. At times, we would rather have stayed and eaten with our friends at school. Sometimes, when we got back, sides were drawn and games were underway, and we had to find our own activities for noon recess.

One day, my cousin Ray walked to his home at noon, too. He lived three quarters of a mile east of school; we lived a quarter mile west. At home, he pulled some fat carrots from his mother's garden, and gnawed on them while he put a halter on his pet steer, then led it down the gravel road to school. I was coming back and met him at the driveway

"Why are you bringing Hayseed to school?' I asked.

"He wanted to come to school, too." Ray grinned, scratching the steer between its horns. "Do you think we could get him into the schoolhouse?"

"Sure, I'll help," I volunteered. Ray pulled two ears of corn from the pockets of his bib overalls, and we nine-year-olds went to work. I set the corn on the first of five steps and waited breathlessly as Ray quietly led the steer to the golden bait. As they approached, I moved it a step higher. The steer snorted nervously, but followed the corn. Another step, I moved it again. Its hooves scraped and slid awkwardly as it strove to maintain a footing on the concrete steps. Ray kept one hand tightly on the rope around the steer's neck, and with his other hand, patted Hayseed's shoulder, calming him in his struggle to reach the delectable morsel. Before long, we had an audience. Swings emptied, jump ropes sprawled in grass, and baseball gloves dropped as students became absorbed in the drama.

"Shhh," Ray cautioned, "Don't spook 'im, or he'll run."

Speaking softly to his steer, Ray patiently coaxed it until, tail twitching, Hayseed finally reached the top step. "Careful now, open the door and move the corn into the cloak room," Ray instructed in barely a whisper.

We were about to cross the threshold into the entry-way when, "Ding, ding-a-ling!" The teacher stepped out, vigorously ringing the brass school bell to call the students inside. It was hard to tell who was more startled, the children, the city-bred teacher or the five hundred pound Hereford! Hayseed broke free of Ray's grasp, bolted down the steps and across the schoolyard, but not before plopping giant green "Pies" on the steps as calling cards.

Ray took off in pursuit of his steer, finally caught it, and tied it to a tree. He paused for a moment, then ran back for the corn and dropped it in front of his pet. Meanwhile, Teacher carefully steered the children up the messy steps and settled them down to begin afternoon classes. When Ray walked in late, she snapped, "Use the shovel from the coal room to clean up the mess." Then added, "And wash it at the pump when you're finished!

Ray got back just in time for arithmetic class. Stifling a giggle, he whispered, "Hayseed wouldn't have made a mess if he hadn't been frightened at the sound of that darn bell!"

At afternoon recess, Teacher announced," You're all excused to go out and play, except Faye and Ray. When everyone was outside playing, Teacher said, "You two will do the arithmetic problems on page thirty-eight!" The crack of bat against ball and singsong chants of girls skipping rope floated through open windows while Teacher lectured us.

"And Faye," she added indignantly. "You're a girl, and girls just don't do this sort of thing!"

We two renegades sneaked a glance at each other's freckled faces and grinned, as if to say, "The fun was well worth the trouble."

Duke and Dolly

ഇരു

Carol and I were playing cops and robbers with our brothers Dick, Jerry, and Dennis, when Daddy drove into the yard. A cattle truck followed him and parked by the barn door.

We tossed aside the wooden sticks we were using for guns and gathered around the truck, wondering if we were going to ship an animal to the stockyards in South St. Paul. "Nah," Dick said. "The trucker has to be here at six o'clock in the morning to do that. This one's delivering something!"

We wondered what was inside as the driver swung down from the cab and strode to the back of the truck. Shuffling and snorting sounds emanated from inside as he pulled out the loading chute and opened the door, then stepped inside. He spoke quietly to the animals, then reappeared, leading a big brown work horse down the chute. Daddy stood by the horse's head and held its bridle while the trucker went back inside and brought out another horse almost identical to the first one.

"Get back!" Daddy commanded. "They might be nervous." We all stepped back except Dick, who opened the barnyard gate so Daddy could lead them inside. They snorted softly as he unbuckled their bridles and slapped them gently on the neck.

Sensing their freedom, they headed straight for the water tank, their big hooves clopping on the rocky ground. The muscles rippled in their powerful haunches, and the coarse hair of their manes and tails swished when they walked.

I climbed the board fence and watched them drink. Their brown eyes, fringed with thick lashes, were high and off to the side of their long, slim heads. I thought they were beautiful, but too big and frightening for me. They dipped their soft muzzles into the water tank and noisily skimmed long, drawn-out slurps of water. When they finally had their fill, the water was an inch lower in the tank.

When the trucker left, Mama came outside to see the horses. "What are their names?" she asked.

"This one's Dolly, and that one's Dick," Daddy answered.

Mama glanced at her son's crestfallen face and said, "I think one Dick in the family is enough." Then she announced firmly, "From now on, they'll be called Duke and Dolly."

I stood on my perch on the fence and watched them for a long time, wondering if I'd ever get over being afraid of horses.

At least, I thought, *they're safely inside, and I'm safely outside the fence.*

Daddy liked using his horses for making hay. One day, Carol and I saw him and the boys coming across the field with a full load. The hayrack undulated over the ruts, swaying to the rhythm of the horses' gait as they slowly pulled it home. We ran across the stubbly meadow, grabbed the braces on the back of the rack and hitched a ride.

Daddy drove the team to the shady north side of the barn and called out, "Whoa!" He wound the reins around the post on the rack and climbed down. "We'll unload after lunch," he said. Turning around, he noticed me and said, "Faye, watch the horses," then strode into the house to eat.

I was afraid of horses and ashamed to tell my dad of my fears. He would have asked, "Are you a baby? If you are, then stay in the house with Mama!" I stayed with the horses, but stood as far away as I dared.

What would I do if they started to run? I stood off to the side just to be safe. The noonday sun bore down as I waited for what seemed like hours for the meal to end and someone, anyone, to come outside and watch the horses with me.

The horses snorted and rippled their skin when flies landed on them. Occasionally they shook their manes and lifted a great, clopping hoof. Afraid they would walk away, I barked Whoa!" in my fiercest eight-year-old voice.

Through the screen door, I could hear dishes rattling and snippets of conversation around the kitchen table. Daddy might be telling stories about his corn-husking days in Iowa when he was a young man. He still had his husking harness, rusty now from disuse. It was a leather strap with a metal hook attached that fit over his right hand. He would slit dry husks down the ear of corn, then pull them off by hand. He and his friends used to race to see who would be the first to fill a wagon box with golden ears. Or, maybe he was talking about his army days in 1918. He might even be telling my favorite story, the one about the time he climbed all the way to the top of the Statue of Liberty, right up to the torch!

When the horses tossed their manes to chase away flies, their harnesses jingled. I shouted "Whoa!" even louder, with one eye on the kitchen door, hoping someone would come out to relieve me, but no one seemed to notice. A kitten came by and I picked it up, burying my neck in its downy fur. When the harnesses rattled again, I yelled even louder, frightening the kitten which scampered away.

After Daddy had his last cup of coffee, he'd usually scrape his chair back and reach into his bib overall pocket for his can of Copenhagen snuff. He'd twist the shiny tin cover open, reach in, take a pinch between his thumb and forefinger and wedge it inside his bottom lip. Then the meal would be over.

Finally Daddy and the boys came out! I raced to the house in relief, and Mama set a place for me at the table. While Bernice and Jean washed the dishes, I ate my lunch and boasted to my siblings, "I was watching Duke and Dolly!"

I didn't tell them how scared I was. My secret was still safe.

The Project

Awakening to the smell of bacon sizzling, the clatter of dishes and the reassuring sounds of Mama's voice in the kitchen, I stretched and wondered if the hole would still be there. Slipping out of bed quietly so as not to awaken my two little sisters, I pulled a cotton dress made of flowered feed sacks over my skinny shoulders and walked into the kitchen. Daddy was already at work, and Mama was kneading a batch of bread in the huge aluminum pan that usually hung on a nail behind the stove, while Jean and Bernice made breakfast.

The screen door slammed behind me as I walked down the narrow wooden steps and around the corner of the house. There it was, a twelve by twelve-foot-square dugout with a mountain of dirt alongside. With arms folded across my chest, I stood at the edge and stared into the hole, then walked part way up the pile, surveying the tracks made by my bare feet. The dirt was still soft and cool, and when I wiggled my toes, it squeezed between them like little brown anthills. Yesterday, my brothers and sisters and I watched in awe as the noisy machine bit off chunks of hard ground and spit it out, soft and gravelly onto an ever growing pile. *The ground is hard enough to hold trains and churches, but it comes out so soft. I wonder how that can be*, I mused, and lazily wandered back to the kitchen door to sit on the steps.

Already the sun was climbing over the barn and it shone warmly on my shoulders as I picked up a dozing kitten. Its soft, downy fur tickled my skin as it nestled against my neck. Close by, the barn doors were open, and I saw my brothers finishing the chores. The calves were bawling hungrily as they poked their heads through the slats in the pen.

Still carrying the kitten, I stepped inside the cool interior. The familiar barn smells were comfortable in my nostrils: animals, waste, the fermenting odor of corn silage, and the sweet smell of clover hay. I put the kitten down and poured milk into the cats' dish, a dented aluminum frying pan, then called, "Here kitty, kitty." Instantly seven or eight cats came running; some scampered from the hayloft, others from the farmyard. They crouched in a circle around the pan, heads touching, tails twitching, and silently lapped the milk.

The hay and straw, strewn on the cool dirt floor, felt good under my feet as I petted the hungry calves. "Wanna feed one?" thirteen-year-old Dick asked as he mixed the milk and poured it into pails.

"Sure!" I held the pail as the calf drank, slurping, snorting and butting its head too far into the pail. I had to hold it tightly or the calf would tip it over and lose his breakfast. With my other hand, I kept the other calves away as they bellowed and pushed against each other, trying to get their heads into the same pail. "No, no, you must wait your turn," I laughed. When the calf reached the bottom of the pail, it continued to lick and slurp until I reluctantly pulled it away.

Then, I helped Dennis open the stanchions to let the seven milk cows out of the barn. They backed across the gutter and filed, one by one, through the narrow door into the rocky barnyard. Blinking in the bright sunlight, the cattle headed straight for the gate that leads to the pasture. Dennis opened the gate while I shooed them through. It took both of us to close it. Together, we set the gatepost inside the wire loop of the adjoining fence post. I pushed against it with all my might while Dennis slipped the wire loop around the top to hold the gate securely in place.

Mama called "Breakfast is ready! Wash up before you come in." We all trooped to the well, one pumping the cold water while the rest scrubbed their hands under the flow. When we came in for breakfast, Mama said, "Let's pray." She and her children folded their hands and began. "Bless us, oh Lord and these thy gifts.. ." before enjoying a meal of salt pork, scrambled eggs and homemade bread spread with Karo syrup, and washed down with a glass of fresh foamy milk.

While we ate, Mama, a petite, dark-haired young woman, discussed the plans for today's project. "With everyone's help," she said, "We'll start laying the fieldstone walls for the cellar." It will go under the addition Daddy will build onto the tiny farmhouse. "We'll put up boards for forms, and then fill them with cement and rocks."

After breakfast, everyone except the toddlers was given a job. Jean, the eldest, stoked the fire in the already warm kitchen, filled the teakettle and set it on the stove to heat for washing breakfast dishes. She and Bernice will also sweep the kitchen and bake fat, glossy loaves of bread out of the dough that is rising in the big pan.

Dick and Jerry harnessed the horse to bring up a load of rocks from the pile in the field. "Hold Dolly's halter while we harness her," Dick called to me. Always afraid of horses, but not wanting my big brother to think I was chicken, I came to the side of the barn. He overturned a wooden crate in front of the huge animal and I stepped up on it, reached up and gingerly grasped the leather strap along Dolly's face. I flinched, but hung on as Dolly snorted and tossed her head when Dick slipped the bit into her mouth, rolling the steel rod across her tongue and past long yellow teeth. "Whoa," he said softly, "Whoa." He stood on tiptoe to slide the collar onto her shoulders, and then slapped the heavy harness over her back. Connecting the reins to her bridle, he stood behind her and gently pulled back on them. "Back, Dolly, back." The big animal obeyed, and the boys deftly hooked the stone boat chains to her traces. Relieved to let go of the bridle, I stepped down from my perch and moved it aside as Dick slapped the reins lightly across the horse's rump and stepped into the stone boat with Jerry. It slid down the path behind the horse like a giant sled.

"What's my job, Mama?" I asked, returning to the house and hoping I wouldn't be sent inside to wipe the breakfast dishes.

"Play with the little ones," Mama said, "Keep them away so they don't fall into the hole." I put Mary Ann and Walt into the red wagon and pulled them to the barn.

"Wanna play with the kitties?" I asked. The babies tumbled in the straw, squealing in delight as the shy kittens scrambled from their pudgy grasp. They stopped to pet the calves but pulled away as the smallest calf licked their fingers with its scratchy tongue. Back in the Red Flyer, I pulled them to the warm brooder house where a yellow mass of fluffy, week old chicks darted between feeders and water fonts.

"Wanna catch a peep-peep!" the little ones insisted.

"No, no," I cautioned, but cupped one in my hands and brushed it against their soft cheeks. Then, I took them into the house for safekeeping, because Mama called me to carry water for the cement trough, a rectangular wooden box that was used to mix the cement for the walls.

Everyone was excited about the project and eager to be helping. A homemade wooden ladder was lowered into the dugout, and Mama and Dick descended into the hole. Jerry took a garden hoe and mixed gravel, concrete and water in long sweeping motions until it looked like grainy, gray cake batter. Then, pail by pail, he scooped the heavy cement mixture from the trough and handed it down to Mama who poured it into the forms. Carol, Dennis, and I kept busy carrying rocks to the edge where we carefully rolled them to our oldest brother. He plopped them into the thick dollops of concrete that oozed between each layer.

More water had to be pumped and carried. Carol and I raced with our pails, cold water sloshing on bare feet. "I won!" "No, I did!" we argued. Hot and thirsty, we cupped our hands under the spout and tried to drink from them but the water drained through our fingers.

"Pump slowly," I instructed as I put my mouth under the faucet, but Carol pulled down hard on the pump handle and cold water gushed over my face and into my nostrils. Choking and sputtering, I wiped the water out of my eyes, grabbed a pail and doused Carol with it.

"Water fight!" Dennis yelled, and jobs were forgotten as a half-dozen siblings joined in the melee. When Mama put an end to it, we returned to work, dripping but cool.

At noon, Mama said, "You've all done a good job. We're half finished with the first wall." After lunch, some played Hide and Seek while Mama glanced through the St. Cloud Times, which came through the noon mail. Carol and I played with paper dolls.

Then it was back to work. By mid afternoon, water carrying was tiresome, rocks got heavier, and children bickered. As usual, Mama tried to distract us with her stories. "Did I ever tell you about when I was a little girl..." she began."I was only about nine years old," she continued, "About your age, Dennis, when my dad let me take the horse and buggy by myself for the first time.

I went to visit my cousins and stopped in the woods along the way to pick some chokecherries. It was a hot, still day, no birds singing, just the sound of flies buzzing, and I was all alone in that big woods. All of a sudden, there was a rustle in the brush. My heart stopped, as I was sure I saw the brown furry coat of a bear in the distance! Well! Berries scattered everywhere as I raced for the buggy. I slapped the reins against Prince's back and he galloped to the safety of the open road! There were no chokecherries for my cousins that day!"

I liked Mama's horse stories. *I wish I was as brave as Mama,* I thought. *I wish I could drive Dolly to the woods or sit on her and ride like a cowboy, but Duke and Dolly are so big, they're noisy when they slurp water from the tank, and they have such big, clopping hooves, I'm always afraid they'll step on my feet if I get too close.* I liked riding on the hayrack when they pulled it, but I was still afraid of Duke and Dolly.

Late in the afternoon, as Mama reached up to set the last of the stones into the opening, it rolled against her hand and her fingers were pinched between two rocks. We could see the pain on Mama's face as she cupped her bruised hand. After lifting heavy rocks and concrete all day, the pain was made more intense by exhaustion, causing big tears to run down her cheeks. "Everybody has worked hard today and we're all tired," she said through her tears. "We'll stop for today. Boys, rinse the cement trough; and girls, put the pails back in the barn. We all did as she asked, subdued by her tears.

Later, the boys started evening chores and Mama called me to bring the vegetables from the garden, "Pull the radishes and onions and wash them at the pump." she instructed. Soon, Daddy was home, and supper was on the table. He was surprised to see the fine job we had done. One whole wall completed!

Daddy had built the house five years ago, along with the red barn and a chicken coop, on an eighty-acre clover field that he purchased from his father. Originally, he built the rooms for a granary. "We will live here until I get the new house built." he said. Somehow, he never got around to building the house. A railroad car, later attached to the house, served as bedrooms for the children. A kitchen and a bedroom for Mama and Daddy were the only other rooms.

With the new addition, we would have a living room. Under it, a root cellar would hold apples, cabbage, squash and potatoes for winter. There would be shelves for canned goods, and space for the crocks of brine used to cure hams and bacon at butchering time. Having our own cellar meant we wouldn't have to store all our canned goods and produce at Grandpa's house a half-mile away, and we would have it on hand whenever we needed it.

After supper, Daddy climbed down the ladder into the hole. "This is such a big job," he said, "We'll work on the rest of the walls in the evenings when I'm home." We children were proud of our big accomplishment that day, but along with Mama, we all nodded our heads in agreement. We needed Daddy's muscles to build stone cellar walls!

County Fair

ℰↃ০ℛ

Late one summer afternoon, Mama wiped her hands on her apron and said, "There, I've canned all the pickles I'm going to for this year!" Rows of canned pickles filled the kitchen like green soldiers standing at attention. She had to make enough for the entire year because they took the place of fresh salads during the cold winter months. Even after we had canned all the pickles we needed, the vines sprawled lazily across the garden, their yellow blossoms turning into more cucumbers than the family can consume or give away.

When Daddy came home from work that evening, he decreed, "With all the people starving in the old country, we can't let these pickles go to waste." It was decided that Carol and I would keep the cucumbers picked off the vines. If we did a good job, Daddy would sell them after work, and we'd get the money to spend at the Benton County fair.

The next morning, we were temporarily relieved of our dreaded job of wiping breakfast dishes. Swinging a basket between us, we raced to the garden in the golden morning sunshine. We snapped the torpedo-shaped produce from the vines and joyously plopped them into our basket, in anticipation of overflowing coffers. Within days, however, the project grew tiresome, and we lost interest. Succulent, green cukes were picked for supper each evening, and the rest grew into fat, golden, submarines, creeping across the sun-baked ground, and eventually becoming a treat for the hogs in their pen; and we were back to wiping breakfast dishes.

At last, it was county fair time, the highlight of our summer! For weeks, we children talked of little other than merry-go-rounds and Ferris wheels as we crawled along the endless rows of vegetables in the family garden, pulling weeds and hoeing the caked earth. It was especially exciting this year because at eight and nine years old, it was the first time Carol and I had our own money and were allowed to spend a day at the fair with no adult supervision.

Mama cut thick slices of homemade bread and spread them with butter and fresh chokecherry jelly, wrapped them in cellophane and dropped the packet into a paper bag, then tucked in a few warm oatmeal cookies.

"Don't lose your lunch," she cautioned. "Daddy will pick you up at the main gate at 4:30. Here's your pickle money," she added, tying two quarters and a dime into the corner of a clean cotton handkerchief for each of us. "That should be enough for two rides each and an ice cream cone." Finally, she cautioned, "Be good girls and don't waste your money on shills!"

"We won't! Bye, Mama!" we sang as we raced to the car.

The morning air was cool when Daddy dropped us off at the fairgrounds. Instead of the hustle and bustle we expected, we were disappointed that it was still quiet and sleepy. We wandered aimlessly through the midway, deserted except for an occasional carnival worker quietly tinkering on an engine. Tents were closed and concession stands shuttered. We wandered past the drowsy tilt-a-whirl, its seats leaning drunkenly on the topsy-turvy floor, then past festooned merry-go-round horses frozen rigidly at attention in mid-gallop. How strange it was without the sounds of the calliope, the wheedling barkers or the shrieks of riders whirling in dizzy circles overhead. No multi-colored lights blinked on the rides as generators sat idle, their fat electrical cables slithering from one attraction to another across dusty sand.

We explored the empty grandstand, climbing to the top tier to watch the panorama of the makeshift city unfold like a movie in slow motion. Then, we sauntered to the exhibit area where the grass was thick and green, and stopped at the 4-H building. We looked at the exhibits: a breadboard in the shape of a pig, sawed by a schoolboy with the fine blade of a coping saw. There were cookies, three to a plate, and aprons and dresses, made by the older girls, including our sisters Jean and Bernice. We walked by peach crates containing wilting carrots, kohlrabi, string beans, and tomatoes. The vegetable boxes reminded us of tedious days spent hoeing and weeding, so we moved on, taking a shortcut to the livestock buildings. It was cool in the barns, and peaceful, but we didn't stay long. After all, we didn't come to see farm animals; we could see them at home. We came for excitement! Rides! Noise! And we were anxious for the fun to begin.

By mid morning, our lunch bag was beginning to feel heavy and the chokecherry jelly was soaking through so we found ourselves a cool spot in the shade and ate an early lunch. The chokecherry jelly was refreshingly tart on our tongues as we gobbled down our sandwich. We thought Mama's oatmeal cookies with lots of raisins were the best in the world and ate every last crumb from the bottom of the bag. Before taking another tour of the fairgrounds, we untied our money from the corner of our hanky to check if it was still there. Two quarters and a dime for each of us. We tied it up again and shoved it to the bottom of our pockets, wondering how long we'd have to wait before spending it.

Gradually, the fairgrounds began to stretch and come to life. Canvas tent flaps turned back, and papier-mache dogs, plaster elephants and plush teddy bears stared at us with glassy eyes. These could be ours by simply throwing a ring over a milk bottle or shooting little yellow ducks swimming by! How difficult could that be? But Mama warned us to stay away from them, so we resisted the vendors' coaxing pleas— while staring hungrily at their treasures.

Breezes died and the humidity soared with the sizzling August sun as it crept directly overhead. Stiff blue jeans, new for the school year, clung to our legs like canvas. We were used to running barefoot all summer, and our new leather oxfords made our feet tired and hot. But we didn't care! At last, we were seeing some action! Churning rides! Flashing lights! Blaring music!

Families were everywhere, strollers maneuvering electrical cables like obstacle courses. Cotton candy stuck to faces of children begging for a ride on the merry-go-round. With no one to tell us, "Hurry up, lets go!" Carol and I listened to barkers describe a calf with two heads, a man only two feet tall and a lady with alligator skin. The vivid pictures on the tents piqued our curiosity and sharpened our desire to see these wonders. Neither of us had ever seen an alligator, and we debated whether or not to spend our money to see the scaly woman.

It was a heady experience, not having anyone telling us what to do. No one would decide we were too young to choose the scary rides, or not to dawdle and explore behind the sideshow tents.

On the way to the Ferris wheel, I shouted, "Look at this!" as I pulled Carol under the shade of a canopy, "Steam shovels! Just look at all the good stuff you can win!"

There, in glass cubicles were miniature steam shovels surrounded by treasures too wonderful to resist. Figurines, rings, bracelets and dolls beckoned to us. There were riches for our brothers as well. All one had to do was turn the crank and the machine would clamp its jaws on your favorite trinket. Reel it in and the prize was yours! What could be easier? And it only cost a dime! Anybody could see the stuff was worth a lot more than ten cents. Confidently, we deposited our dimes and started turning the crank.

"I'm going to get the statue of the girl and the dog," I told Carol.

"I'm trying for the bracelet," She answered.

Ever so carefully, we each grasped our prize in the shovel's mouth. Slowly, we turned the crank as it moved jerkily toward its goal. Suddenly the statuette slipped from my shovel's jaws. Again and again I grasped it, only to lose it before I could drop it into the tunnel. Soon, the machine stopped and I needed to deposit another dime. Carol's shovel still clutched the bracelet. She guided it closer to the tunnel. "I think you're going to make it," I whispered. We held our breath, but inches from victory hers too, was lost.

"Let's try it again, this time we'll surely get them," I urged. Over and over we tried, grasping the objects only to drop them.

Finally, Carol said, "I have just enough money to take a ride on the Ferris wheel, want to come with me?"

"You go ahead," I told her, "I'm going to try one more time." When she came back, I was down to my last dime. "I don't have enough money for a ride." I said regretfully, "So I'll try once more. This time, I focused on a pearl handled jackknife, and then my last dime was gone.

The afternoon was a long one with no money to spend. Enviously, we watched the Octopus whirl overhead. We yearned to be among the screaming passengers, scared and thrilled at the same time. Our parched throats longed for the cold velvet of ice cream cones being slurped by folks who didn't waste their money on steam shovels. Our tongues watered as theirs lapped the melting goodness to keep it from trickling down the side of the cone. Hot dog and popcorn aromas tantalized our taste buds and reminded us of our too early lunch.

About 4:00, we headed for the main gate; plopped onto the cool, green grass under a shade tree and waited for Daddy.

"Oh, oh, I just remembered what Mama said," Carol reminded me, "About not wasting our money on shills. What's she gonna say when we tell her?"

"We-ell," I reasoned, "That wasn't exactly a shill; it was a steam shovel." After a moment, I added quietly, "But let's not tell her anyway, OK?"

"OK," she said.

We sat thinking for a long time.

"Know what?" I asked her.

"What?"

"I'm not ever going to try one of those things again!"

"Me neither!" Carol replied.

At last, Daddy drove up and waited with the motor running while we hopped into the back seat. He rarely carried on a conversation with his children, and this was one time we were grateful for the silence as we rode the five miles home.

When we came into the house, Mama was frying fresh side pork in the warm kitchen. The potatoes were boiling, and there was a johnny cake in the oven. Mama told Carol and me to run quickly to the garden and pick a few tomatoes for supper. Later, we were shucking off our hot shoes and blue jeans, when Mama asked, "Did you have a good time at the fair?"

We simply answered, "Yes."

"What did you do?" she asked.

"Nothing," we answered.

The Red Mittens

ⁱ⌃ⁱ

It was late November. The pond was frozen over, and
snow covered the stubble in the cornfields. Winter was
here, and I had no mittens. When I ran down the country road to school in the mornings, I pulled my hands up into
the sleeves of my coat to keep them warm. I hoped to get
mittens for my seventh birthday that fell on Thanksgiving
Day that year.

My birthday finally came, but there were no new mittens. Instead, Mama handed me a skein of red yarn. "This
was left over from tying a quilt," she said. "Dick will knit you
a pair of mittens.

"Red! My favorite color!" I shrieked, burying my fingers and nose in the downy softness.

"When can you start my mittens?" I pestered my eldest and favorite brother.

"As soon as chores are finished this evening," he promised. At 12 years old, Dick is my protector and hero; the one
who taught me how to ride bike, to play dominos and our own
private game of reading backwards.

After supper, I raced through the darkness to the barn
and tagged after my brothers as they finished the chores.
When all the animals were bedded down and the cows
munching sweet clover hay, we left the warmth and stillness
of the barn. Lantern swaying in Dick's hand, we tramped the
short distance back to the house in the crunchy snow.

Once inside, before Dick could remove his boots, I thrust the knitting needles into his hands. "Hold on!" he laughed. "We'll get those mittens made." He took his usual chair at the kitchen table, and in the pale glow of the kerosene lamp, began to cast on stitches. "This will take time," he told me, "I've never knit a pair of mittens before."

Forehead wrinkled in concentration, he counted the stitches, having an equal number on three needles. With the fourth needle, he slowly began to make a cuff—knit two stitches, purl two. Soon his motions became rhythmic: needles click, yarn over, pull through. He was on his way!

Each evening, he picked up the needles and continued where he left off the night before. Each morning I stretched out my hand, and he laid the unfinished mitten atop it to measure his progress. At last one morning when only my fingertips were visible, he exclaimed, "I think I can finish this one tonight!" When I awoke the following morning, one beautiful red mitten was waiting on the kitchen table.

Many mornings later, they were both finished. I gulped down my oatmeal and fidgeted while Mama braided my hair. Finally, it was time for school! I threw on my coat, cap, and overshoes and pulled on my brand new mittens! On the way to school, I made snowballs, and my hands stayed warm. Then, I waved and fluttered my arms like a cardinal in flight, watching those magical red mittens light up the snowy countryside.

One cold morning a few days later, Uncle Ed stopped by with his horses and sleigh. A giant of a man with a full-moon face, he loved to tease and always called me "Giggles." He stepped inside the kitchen door, pulled off his leather mittens and set them on the woodbox. He pushed his foggy glasses onto his broad forehead and stamped snow from his boots.

When he spotted me, he clicked his tongue and poked me playfully with his chubby fingers. "You're gonna freeze out there today, Giggles," he said, good-naturedly. "It's twenty-four below."

"Oh, I won't get cold," I announced, and proudly showed him my red mittens.

He reached for them and teased, "These should fit me. I think I'll keep them," Then he rammed a huge hand into the tiny mitten. I watched in horror as the stitches gave way, and a great hole slowly spread between the thumb and palm of his hand. "Oops!" he said, and hastily peeled the mitten from his hand. "Here you are, Giggles." A glance at Mama's face told him it was time for a quick retreat. He grabbed his own mittens and backed out the kitchen door.

After he left, Dick inspected the frayed mitten as a tear rolled down my cheek. "I think Mama can fix it," he consoled, "but there's no red yarn left."

Mama dug through her quilting supplies and pulled out a ball of brown yarn. "This will have to do," she said. First, she repaired the thumb, and then started on the palm. I watched in dismay as she stitched, in and out, in and out, until there was an ugly brown patch where the hole had been.

"Anyway, Faye," she smiled sadly, "they'll still keep your hands warm."

They did keep my fingers warm, but from that moment, the magic was gone from my beautiful red mittens.

A Letter to Hank

ℰℭℜ

D ear Uncle Hank,

      I need to tell you about all the things that have taken place since you went away.

      We were in town the evening it happened. When school was over, Mama and I rode into St. Cloud with our teacher, Mrs. Schultz. We did our shopping and met Daddy at the White Bear when he got off work. He spent a dime for a glass of beer, drank it, and we began the five mile drive home in darkness, on that cold Minnesota evening in late November.

      We passed Benny's Lunch on the east side of town and were approaching the railroad tracks when we saw the revolving lights of a police car at the scene of an accident.

      "Why, that's Hank's car!" Daddy exclaimed. The policeman was directing traffic and motioned for us to keep going, but Daddy coasted to the curb and got out. I stood up in the backseat and craned my neck to watch his silhouette as he strode to the accident scene. A neon light from the gas station across the street, glinted against the familiar blue hood of your crumpled 1938 Ford; its front end hoisted to a wrecker, ready to be towed away. The rotating lights of the police car flickered eerily on and off their faces as Daddy spoke to the policeman, their breaths a cloud of vapor each time the beacon spiraled in their direction.

"They've taken Hank to the hospital," Daddy said as he pulled back into traffic. I huddled alone in the back seat and listened to my parents anxiously discuss your unknown condition, as we drove down the dark country road.

At home, they told my ten brothers and sisters about the accident, and then left instructions. "Keep the fires going," they said. "Do the chores and put the little ones to bed, then pray for Hank!" With that, they left abruptly for the hospital. They would drive the half-mile out of their way to your farm and take Aunt Teen with them. I felt like I had pebbles in my stomach, and I wished Mama could be home with us, as I watched the beam of headlights cut a swath through the dark farmyard, arch at the driveway, and disappear down the gravel road.

Frightened and subdued, we ate supper and did our evening chores without the teasing and bickering that usually goes on when our parents aren't home. The boys lit the lantern and went out to milk our seven cows and feed the calves, while we girls washed the dishes, swept the kitchen and put the little ones to bed. That night, we didn't make fudge, or chop ice from the stock tank to freeze homemade ice cream, as we usually do when our parents go away. Instead, after the wood box was filled, and a pail of fresh drinking water brought in, we knelt by mismatched, wooden kitchen chairs and prayed the rosary for you, our favorite uncle, who was like a second father to us.

Then, Jean the oldest at sixteen, blew out the flame in the kerosene lamp that sat on the middle of the kitchen table, and we went to bed. We fell asleep to the sounds of embers crackling in the wood-burning heater, each snuggled next to a younger sibling, who had heated our bed like an oven.

It was late when Mama and Daddy came home, and we awoke to the sound of crying. We stood around the kitchen and listened in fright as Mama told us that your chest was crushed by the impact of the collision, and you died before reaching the hospital. "When we saw him," she added, "He didn't look dead, just very peaceful, like he was asleep." Daddy's face was ashen and his eyes glistened, as he told us he'd lost his brother and best friend. He said now that the war was over, you and he had been looking forward to better times for our country.

One by one, the family drifted back to bed, grateful to be sleeping next to someone, not wanting to be alone. Into the night, we heard the sounds of our parents' quiet discussion, their droning voices finally comforting and lulling us to sleep.

Is it real? Did Hank really die? Eight-year-old Carol and I wondered as we awoke the next morning. We lay under the warm covers listening to the sounds that mingled with the smells of coffee and wood smoke from the kitchen. "Not Hank!" we declared, "We have too much fun with him!"

Most of our relatives live close by, but you were special to us. You lived on Grandpa's big farm with your wife, Teen, and two daughters, Agnes and baby Margie. I loved spending time on your farm, and nine-year-old Agnes was my partner in mischief. You were patient with us, even when we disobeyed; like the time we were herding your cows in the meadow, and read Agnes' beautiful storybooks instead of watching the cattle. Soon all fifty head of milk cows were grazing on succulent, new shoots of corn in the adjacent field. You patiently explained, "We can't have the cattle trampling the corn, or we won't have a crop next fall." We tried harder, but you understood when Mother Goose and the Brothers Grimm won the battle for our attention, and we were soon relieved of our job.

Sometimes we played rodeo in your calf pen. We tried to ride the baby calves because the older ones were too strong and fast, and would buck us into the dirt. "The younger calves just aren't strong enough to carry an eight-year-old," you cautioned us.

"Besides, you don't belong in that dirty calf pen!" Since you didn't actually forbid us to ride the calves, we didn't tell you, but we still play rodeo now and then.

Mostly, I loved riding on your red, Farmall H tractor as you cultivated row after row of corn in a field that stretched to the horizon. A huge, yellow umbrella was attached to the tractor, keeping the driver cool and shaded, even on the hottest summer days. "Watch the corn," you'd say, "And let me know if it gets covered." I felt important to be helping you—but all too soon, I'd ask to be put off to run and play with Agnes.

"I wish it wasn't Hank!" Carol and I whispered again to each other, then slipped out of bed and brought our clothes to the kitchen to dress by the warm stove.

The next day, your body, dressed in your blue Sunday suit, was brought out to Grandpa's farmhouse, where you lived all your life. A double parlor stretches across the entire front of the house, is used only for rare, special occasions. The few sparse furnishings were moved from one end to make room for the casket. A portable satin screen stood in front of the south window as a backdrop for your coffin. It was flanked by candlesticks that towered above my head, with six candles on each. By evening, in the flicker of candlelight, the aroma of melting beeswax mingled with that of the roses, chrysanthemums, daisies, and gladioli that lined the room.

The evening shadows turned to darkness, and a pall hung over the house. I stayed at your house to be with Agnes. At suppertime, nobody ate much, except the hired man who worked all day and still had three hours of work in the barn. The cows had to be milked, and the cream separated. The calves and pigs needed feeding, and he must tend to the horses and bed down the livestock. Conversation was stilted around the table, as he self-consciously swallowed his food and slurped his coffee.

That evening and the next, your friends, relatives and neighbors, dressed in their Sunday best, came calling to pay their last respects. After the dishes were washed and put away, Agnes and I stood at the window peering into the darkness as cars began to stream into the farmyard. One by one headlights dipped as they crossed the hump in the driveway at the end of the road. The first ones pulled up and parked close to the house in neat rows. Keys were left dangling in ignitions as they slammed car doors and greeted each other on the open porch. Latecomers parked helter-skelter in any available space.

Uncles and aunts visited in hushed tones as they greeted streams of mourners. Friends, neighbors, and close and distant relatives filled the large farmhouse. Most neighbors dropped off a few sandwiches, a cake, or a jar of pickles as they walked through the spacious kitchen.

Besides family and friends, the blacksmith was there, the men from the feed store, and the bartender from the White Bear. You became friends with him on your regular stops for a glass of beer whenever you went to town. The implement dealer was there, too. He sold you the tractor you drove when most of your neighbors were still doing fieldwork with horses. The big rooms were filled with people. With all the bodies pressed closely, the usually chilly rooms were warm and stuffy. Men loosened their ties and unbuttoned their collars and suit jackets, which were worn over long woolen underwear. Used to being outdoors in all weather, their red faces and shiny foreheads betrayed their discomfort.

As usual, Grandpa didn't talk much. Well into his eighties, he had recently moved off the farm to his retirement house in town. He was dressed in his one, black, Sunday suit with a crisp, white shirt and black tie, a felt bedroom slipper on his left foot where he was missing the big toe. He sat stiffly on a straight back chair; gnarled, arthritic hands folded in his lap, and his cane propped against the wall behind him. When condolences were extended, with downcast eyes under bushy white brows, he quietly murmured, "It should have been me."

We children were dutifully marched into the front room by our mothers and aunts to pay our respects. The sweet scent of flowers was strong in my nostrils and reminded me of Grandma's funeral when I was in the first grade. Now, four years later, I didn't realize it was the flowers I smelled, but thought it was the scent of death. You looked so different in the casket that I hardly recognized you. You always had a smile as you gently pulled our pigtails, winked and teased us, and now you were so still. Your normally wavy hair was combed severely back, and your face looked thinner without the customary wad of tobacco in your cheek. We were instructed to say a "Hail Mary" and then stood self-consciously in front of your bier, relieved when we were finally allowed to melt into the crowd.

Our mothers cried, and hugged Agnes. "You poor girl," they said. "You lost your daddy!" Spirited and mischievous by nature, Agnes was unaccustomed to receiving physical affection from adults, but she, too, cried as she stood awkwardly in their embrace. Hugs were mostly given to infants, and we were uncomfortable as we witnessed the rare display of affection.

Sensing the somber mood, we cousins didn't play our usual noisy games, but milled about among the adults. We tried to stay out of our mothers' way as they set stacks of sandwiches, pickles and huge slices of cake on the kitchen table, along with rows of big, white coffee cups. Meanwhile, the aroma of strong black coffee wafted through the house from large, speckled, gray pots that simmered on the wood-burning cook stove.

Now and then, a fifteen-year-old would be sent to the woodpile for another armful of wood, or to the pump for a pail of water for more coffee. He would ask a brother or cousin to accompany him, because it was a night when even the "big boys" were reluctant to venture into the looming darkness alone.

Before the evening was over, the unimaginable would happen—I had to make a trip to the outhouse! Having to go outside to the toilet after dark was bad enough on an ordinary night. However, this evening, with you laying so still in the parlor, and the spirit of death about, the thought of venturing outside alone, crossing the yard, and following the narrow path to where the toilet sat behind the granary, was more than I could fathom.

One by one, I begged my sisters and cousins to go with me, but they were as frightened as I was, and firmly declared, "I don't have to go!" Finally, I could wait no longer. Coatless, and numb with fright, I tore across the farmyard!

It was a cold, clear night, with frost glistening like diamonds on the dead grass. The moon cast sinister figures between the black silhouettes of the closely parked cars, where I thought any manner of evil might be lurking. Was something following me? I imagined being chased, but was too frightened to look over my shoulder. If anything was after me, it would have had to been mighty fleet of foot to catch me! When I reached the outbuildings, shadows obliterated the path I loved to explore in daylight. It was now enclosed in the scary fingers of darkness, and they seemed to be grasping at me from all sides.

The toilet was cloaked in blackness as I felt for the latch and opened the door, then inched my way to the two-holed bench. My breath came in gasps, and the pounding of my heart sounded like a locomotive in my ears. With fingers reluctant to cooperate, I tried to navigate the buttons on the flap of the long underwear covering me from neck to ankles that I wore under my dress and petticoat, as well as the garter belt that hung like a harness from my shoulders to hold up long white stockings.

When finished, without stopping to button up, I kicked open the door and left it swinging agape, as I flew back to safety! Near the house, the soft glow of lamp light beckoning through the kitchen window eased my fears, and I slowed down to catch my breath. Finally, my feet touched the creaking boards of the open porch, and with the reassuring sound of voices in my ears, I quickly stepped into the security of the warm kitchen.

Inside, the entire gathering was kneeling, either on the horsehair carpet in the front room, the wooden floorboards in the dining room, or on the kitchen linoleum, to pray the rosary. Older cousins, girls in their early teens, were chosen to kneel in front of the casket and lead the prayers. I took my place beside my small cousins as we offered our prayers for you, asking Mary, the mother of God, to pray for you and for all of us, now and at the hour of our death.

Finally, lunch was eaten, and after shaking hands a last time, departures were taken, and the crowd dwindled. When we had a moment alone, Agnes, Carol and I stood by your casket. "Did you touch my dad?" Agnes asked.

"No," we replied, cringing, "Did you?"

"Yes," she said as she touched you again. Carol and I gingerly extended a forefinger and touched the back of your hand, then hastily withdrew it in surprise. We had expected your flesh to feel warm and pliable, but it was hard and stiff and cold.

"It feels like wood!" I said.

"Yes, I know," Agnes said, but didn't pull her hand away.

After the wake, Daddy drove us home but came back for an all-night vigil at your side. Your brother, Leo, was there, too, and some of your cousins and brothers-in-law. Your sisters stayed up late into the night. It was a close, sharing time for your family, in the house where they all grew up. Later, your sisters, Louise, Loretta, Sr. Hilde, and Marie went to bed, but the men stayed up all night, as it was the custom not to leave the body unattended. The following night the family would repeat the ritual.

On the morning of the funeral, the hearse arrived, and your coffin was closed and taken to St. Augustine's little basement church. During the funeral mass, it seemed strange to hear Father Louis call you "Henry," He said you never missed mass on Sunday. "No matter how busy Henry was, he always had time for church."

When the funeral mass was over, we drove in procession to Assumption cemetery, gathered around your open grave, and prayed again that God would take your soul to Paradise. The November wind blew cold across the bleak skies, and we shivered like the leafless trees on the horizon. After the prayers, we all took turns sprinkling holy water over your casket before it was lowered into the ground.

Later, back at the farm, we warmed ourselves by the big space heater in the dining room where we came together to eat the funeral dinner. After dinner, folks sat in the front room, which became a parlor again. The waning November sunlight filtered through the lace curtains onto the empty space where your coffin stood a few hours earlier. Conversations resumed, almost normally—except for the gap left by the absence of your teasing, jovial manner.

In late afternoon, when the women finished the dishes, they took off their aprons and joined the others in the parlor. Conversations became more animated, and children drifted in to be close to their mothers.

Used only for important family occasions, this was the final one for our family. With you no longer here to do the farm work, Grandpa's farm will be sold to strangers, and it will become the end of an era.

I miss you, and hope you are happy in Heaven.

Your niece, Faye

Snow Storm

࿐

On Sunday afternoon, a menacing darkness loomed low in the sky and blotted out the sun. The air was gray, turning cold and still. Without benefit of radio to predict the weather, Daddy knew instinctively that a snowstorm was brewing off to the west.

By suppertime it was snowing, the flakes driven by a strong northwest wind. Daddy stood outside in the gathering dusk and watched the storm approach. When he came in, he announced, "After supper, I'll walk into town so I don't miss work tomorrow. I'll leave the car here. It'll never make it through the snow."

Grandpa had recently moved to St. Cloud, along with aunt Loretta. Daddy would stay with them in their big stucco house on the corner of 17th Avenue North and walk to work at the Great Northern car shops in Waite Park. When the storm was over, he'd walk back home. He bundled his slim body warmly in a flannel shirt and blue jeans over a heavy union suit. After he buttoned a sweater over his shirt, he pulled on a pair of bib overalls. Then he slid his feet into a pair of four-buckle overshoes, tucking pant legs inside. Finally, he shrugged into his flannel-lined denim jacket and put the earflaps down on his red and black cap. Just before he walked out the door, Mama tied a muffler over his face. Then, with lunch pail in hand and facing the blizzard, he began the five-mile walk to Grandpa's.

That evening while Mama, Jean, and Bernice did the dishes and the boys finished the barn chores, Carol, Kenny, and I brought in water for drinking and filled the teakettle and the reservoir on the stove. Then we filled the woodbox extra full. It was exciting for us to be out in the swirling snow, and with our older brothers nearby in the quiet barn, we were in no hurry to go back into the house.

Later that evening, Mama predicted there would be no school tomorrow. When we heard this news, we knew we could stay up a little later. "Let's make ice cream!" we begged, and she consented. While Dick and Jerry chopped ice from the water tank, she stirred up the ice cream. We turned it in the kitchen, then had a delicious treat before bedtime.

The next day we awoke to a blizzard that howled in rage around our door. Waves of wind-driven snow bore their way into crevices and piled up in swirling mounds across the fields. Our wood-burning heater was not sufficient to warm the cold floors, and our house was cold and drafty in the strong wind. When the outside chores were finished, we huddled around the heater.

"It's a good day to make Christmas cookies!" Mama announced. "We'll make cutout cookies, white ones and our nice brown Kris Kringles." She mixed the batter and rolled the dough into thin sheets on our small kitchen counter. We soon forgot about the cold as we cut out and baked hundreds of elephants, angels, stars, and gingerbread men. In the evening, we'd frost and decorate them. It was our favorite Christmas tradition.

After supper, we stirred up confectioner's sugar and milk to make big bowls of white icing. We had lots of colored sugars, silver balls, and colorful sprinkles to trim the cookies. After the little ones were in bed, the rest of us sat around the kitchen table and worked on the project. Mama showed us how to take a pinch of colored sugar between our thumb and forefinger and strew it in a narrow line like a paintbrush on the white frosting. We tried to follow her artistic suggestions so ours would be the cookies chosen to hang on the Christmas tree. Sometimes we accidentally broke a leg off a camel or a reindeer. "Oh, dear, the cookie is broken, we'll have to eat it!" we said joyfully. But we always had to share it with the person next to us. With the storm raging outside, and the teakettle whistling softly in the quiet kitchen, it was a good time for stories, jokes, and conversation.

During snowstorms, we played checkers, old maid, and other card games, or put the Tinkertoys and Lincoln logs on the kitchen table to build things. On those evenings, Mama usually set aside her sewing and other chores. Instead, she'd join our games or make fudge or popcorn balls for us.

When the storm had finally spent itself, we awoke to the sun's brilliance on a world, hushed and white with snow. Except for the wispy contrails of smoke from a chimney in the distance, we seemed to be the only inhabitants in a pristine wonderland. We couldn't wait to go outside and play in snow that covered everything and muffled sounds so that our voices echoed in the stillness. Crystal icicles hung from eaves, and snow banks curved like frozen crests of ocean waves. Others looked like sand dunes, so cold and crisp we could walk across them without breaking the crust.

Roads were still closed, and life was at a standstill. While the rest of the world was digging out, we children had an entire day to enjoy nature's bountiful gift of snow. We would make caves, shovel paths, slide downhill, and play games. Tonight, Daddy would walk back home, and tomorrow the roads would be plowed. Then Teacher could get through, so we'd be back in school. Today the world was ours.

A Trip to the Cities

ഇരുള

Daddy now worked for the railroad as a carman at the Great Northern car shops in Waite Park. By repairing boxcars for a living, he would have a steady income to feed his family and wouldn't have to rely entirely on the proceeds from the eighty-acre farm. Another advantage of his new job was that he and his family could ride free on Great Northern trains.

Christmas was coming, and Mama promised Carol and me a pre-holiday trip to the twin cities! Can we go tomorrow?" Carol begged.

"No," Mama shook her head, "We will go next Tuesday." Carol and I eagerly counted off the six days until we would ride the train for the first time.

Tuesday morning, Mama tiptoed into our room at 5:00 a.m. and nudged us awake. "Bring your clothes into the kitchen so you don't awaken your sisters," she whispered. We scrambled out of bed and dressed quietly by lamplight in front of the warm kitchen stove while Mama packed Daddy's lunch for work. Instead of the usual pigtails in our hair, she put it in curlers last night, so we took the curlers out and combed through it, impatient to be on our way, and glad we didn't have to stand still while mama braided it. Before we stepped out the door, Mama stoked the fires, then cupped her hand behind the top of the lamp chimney and blew across it, leaving the kitchen in darkness. Carol and I ran across the frigid yard toward the lights of the waiting car, and our adventure began!

Daddy drove us to the Great Northern depot in the crisp, pre-dawn darkness of the cold winter day where we would catch the 6:05 a.m. train to Minneapolis.

The platform trembled and the engine whistled loudly as the train rolled up to the station. Along with a dozen or so other passengers, we stood close enough to touch it when the screech of brakes brought it to a halt. Bell clanging and ponderous bulk quaking, it hissed and snorted like a one-eyed dragon anxious to pursue its prey. The rhythmic lever on the middle wheel, continued to move up and down, warning us of the brevity of this stop.

With every puff of the engine, smoke billowed from the stack, and a whoosh of steam wrapped us in a thick fog, reducing the station lights to a glimmer. The dim, naked bulb in the platform's overhead lamp squinted through the fog and cast eerie shadows on huddling passengers. The flicker of a lantern seemed to be swinging from a phantom hand as a switchman walked in a steamy blur alongside the conveyance. The most impressive light was the beacon on the front of the train, a single huge globe, like a giant eye in the center of the engine. It flicked its powerful, rotating beam, searching the darkness, and illuminating the rails with laser-like shafts of light.

As we boarded, a uniformed conductor stood by the open door and hustled us up the narrow, portable steps, which he then pulled inside. When the last passenger had entered,

Carol Bromenschenkel, 1944.

77

he leaned out the door and shouted, "All aboard!" Seconds later, the train jerked and lurched forward, wheels click-clacking on the rails. As it gathered momentum, the lights of the station receded into the darkness.

We shivered in anticipation as we settled into the luxurious plush seats, Mama on one side with her purse and the shoebox beside her, Carol and I on the seat facing her. With soft light inside the coach and darkness outside, we looked out the window but saw only the reflection of our own excited faces.

At first, we sat shyly and quietly, lulled by the movement of the train, but in a few moments, curiosity prompted us to investigate our surroundings. "What does this do?" Carol asked, pointing to the button on the armrest.

"It adjusts the back of your seat," Mama explained, then showed us how to raise the leg rest, too. We fidgeted with the seat adjustments and window shade until we were fully acquainted with their functions. Then, hanging on to the backs of seats, we lurched down the aisle of the swaying car, solemnly studying the sleeping passengers, many of whom were soldiers. Most had spent the night on the train; small white pillows under heads, bodies folded on seats too short, nestled under winter coats doubling as blankets. Riders began to stir and sit up as we walked by; they yawned, ran a comb through their hair, or stuffed their feet back into shoes. Some of the soldiers wished us "Good morning", and we shyly mumbled "Morning" in return. Satisfied with our inspection, we finally settled back into our seats, and the conductor came by to punch our pass. He looked very handsome in his navy blue jacket with gold braid and buttons, and a matching blue cap with a shiny black visor. We watched as he punched our pass, then scribbled a number on a card and tucked it into the slot above our seat. He smiled and said, "Enjoy your day, ladies," then disappeared down the aisle. When he was gone, Mama unfolded the plans for the day ahead, and then drifted into tales about her life as a little girl, living near Clear Lake. Her stories made the time pass swiftly, and before we knew it, we reached the cities.

Pulling into the train station in St. Paul, we were in an area where dozens of railroad tracks converged and lay side by side in a vast underground network. Amid puffs of steam hanging low in the air, we disembarked and joined throngs of people pouring from trains that stood like moving walls on each side of us. Leaving the quiet, subdued atmosphere of the train, we stepped onto a noisy walkway bustling with Redcaps loading luggage, and people darting between baggage carts and each other. Everyone seemed to be in a hurry. We were swept along with women, carrying their luggage and hanging onto their children; impatient businessmen, in hats and top coats and carrying brief cases; strident soldiers and sailors with solidly packed duffel bags slung across their backs winding through the crowds, hurrying to catch the next train on their voyage to an unknown destiny. Carol and I wondered who all these people were, and where were they going in such a hurry.

Bells clanged, engines throbbed, and steam hissed all around us. In the noisy confusion, Mama beckoned us to follow her through the crowds and up the stone steps into the immense depot.

Once inside, our footsteps echoed on the granite floors, and the noises of countless passengers reverberated from high ceilings and granite walls. The voice over the public speaker, which announced the arrival and departure of trains, rose above the din. Its unseen monotone droned incessantly with a litany of every stop along the line for each departure, as well as the gate number, time and the railroad's name.

Mama allowed us to dawdle and gawk at the high ceilings, the huge wall clocks, and lines of people at the ticket cages, and then told us we'd take the streetcar to the Minnesota Capitol.

It was still early morning, and people were lined up

Lillian Bromenschenkel, 1944.

waiting for the trolley to take them to their destinations. A squat, tired looking woman in a worn coat, a head scarf tied under her chin, and purse dangling at her side, waited on flat, tired feet to begin another day of cleaning or factory work. Private school students, in crisp uniforms, stood in little groups, with stacks of books under their arms. Young women in perky hats, hosiery seams straight above high heels, tripped hurriedly to jobs in offices and banks, their wide shouldered, knee length coats flaring jauntily at their sides. Stolid workmen, clad in clean overalls and carrying tin lunchboxes were enroute to another day of building automobiles at the Ford plant. We took our place in line and waited with the others.

The streetcar approached on a track and was tethered to an overhead cable, like a legless dog on a leash. It stopped smoothly in front of us, and the door swung open. Coins tinkled into the glass container as Mama deposited our fare into the slot, and we found seats. As it filled up, passengers stood, clutching straps that hung from the ceiling. This was a day of first experiences for Carol and me. We had never ridden a train before, nor had a ride on a streetcar. It was also the first time we had been away from St. Cloud, a city populated predominantly with Germans, Scandinavians and Irish, so we had never seen people of race or skin color other than our own. We soon became part of a diverse cultural mixture of riders; some with smooth, dark skin and kinky hair, some with black hair and almond eyes, others blonde, with round blue eyes, and some faces like our own, brown-eyed and freck-led.

The golden horses were visible from a distance long before we approached the State Capitol at seventy-five Constitution Avenue. We began the steep ascent up the broad steps of the building that Mama told us are made of granite from the St. Cloud quarries. Carol and I began counting steps as we climbed the immense stairway, but half way up, lost count and wanted to start over. Mama said, "No."

Once inside, there was a stillness and sense of rever-ence about the Capitol, and we spoke in whispers. Our foot-steps echoed on the stone floors as we stepped to the center of the rotunda and craned our necks, looking upward into the dome. "The top of the dome is 223 feet up," Mama said, read-ing from a brochure. "It's the largest unsupported marble dome in the world, outside of St. Peter's church in the Vatican."In fact," she said, "I believe Cass Gilbert, the archi-tect, patterned it after the one in the Vatican." We took our time looking at the paintings on the walls and marveled at the smooth elegance of the marble staircases, columns and arches. No one accompanied us, so we quietly explored the building on our own, peeking into an empty courtroom, read-ing the signs over the doors, and admiring paintings depict-ing battles of Minnesota soldiers in the Civil War, while Mama explained various state government functions.

Finally, she said, "It's time to see the golden horses!" This is what we had been waiting for! We took the elevator and stepped out onto the balcony in front of the dome. There, we viewed the quadriga; two young women, four hors-es with heads held high and golden manes flowing, and a young man standing on a chariot pulled by the horses. They were much bigger than we imagined them to be from our position on the street below and we felt small beside them. "They are made of copper, and are covered with twenty-three and a half karat gold leaf, Mama told us, reading again from the brochure. "The four horses represent the powers of nature; earth, wind, fire and water. The two young women represent civilization," she added, "And the man standing on the chariot represents prosperity."

We, too, felt the horses' power as we ran our hands over their sleek muscles and galloping hooves. Suddenly, we discovered initials and other graffiti that visitors had carved into their shoulders and haunches! We asked Mama who caused the damage. "It's hard to say," she said. "I don't understand why anyone would want to do such a thing." The three of us were dismayed and outraged that anyone would damage this beautiful monument.

Soon, Mama turned to the railing and pointed out landmarks on the horizon. In relief, we averted our eyes and looked across the wintry city. "There's the Foshay Tower, the tallest building in Minneapolis," she announced, "We'll go there next!"

Back on the streetcar and feeling like old hands, Mama let us deposit our own fare as we headed for the Foshay Tower. We rode the elevator to the top and surveyed the city from the balcony of its tallest building. This time, we must look downward to see the Capitol horses, shining in the winter sun.

By now, we were getting hungry, so we left the Tower and headed for Woolworth's five and dime. We climbed onto a tall stool at the soda fountain and placed our order. "Do you have orange pop?" I asked the gum-chewing waitress behind the counter. Carol wanted orange, too, and Mama ordered 7-Up. The girl pulled the handle to fill three glasses, plopped a straw into each one, and shoved them across the counter.

"That'll be fifteen cents," she said. Mama paid her, then reached into the shoebox she'd been carrying since we left home, and pulled out a piece of fried chicken for each of us. She told us not to pay attention to the people who stared at us while we chewed on our drumsticks and sipped our beverage. When we were finished, she reached into the box again and handed us each a cookie.

Our hunger satisfied, we walked up and down the aisles. When we got to the toy section, Mama let us take our time inspecting dolls, dishes and coloring books, even though she knew we wouldn't be buying them. A sponge rubber ball caught our eye. It was red on one side and blue on the other, with a band of silver stars around the center. "This would be perfect for playing "Ante, Ante, Over!" I exclaimed.

"Or bouncing and catching on our way to school," Carol added. We bounced it a few times on the floor, then, with a sigh, returned it to the shelf. As we came down the last aisle in the corner of the store, we spied a booth enclosed by a curtain. Upon closer inspection, it proved to be a self-service photograph booth. Mama read the directions, and then had Carol sit on the little bench facing the camera. When she deposited a quarter, it snapped her picture. Then it was my turn. Moments later, a strip of four pictures emerged through a slot for each of us. We begged Mama to do the same for herself, so she had her picture taken, too.

Our next stop was Dayton's Department Store where we joined throngs of shoppers on the sidewalk to watch an animated story of Pinocchio in window after window. We forgot about the crowds and the cold winter air as we wound around the store, seeing Geppetto carve Pinocchio from a slab of wood and send him off to school. We were enchanted by his fairy godmother, and Jiminy Cricket, his conscience, as he falls into one mishap after another,

Faye Bromenschenkel, 1944.

83

to emerge victorious at the end of the story, and become a real boy.

Once inside, we took the elevator to the Christmas floor. Carol and I had never seen anything like it, a whole floor dedicated to Christmas! It was filled with decorated trees, stockings hanging on fireplaces, wreaths, candy canes, and toys. We had no idea there were so many pretty Christmas things in the world! In the center of the room, on a large ramp decorated with glistening 'snow,' Santa sat on a throne in regal splendor. Although my twelve-year-old brother, Dick, told me Santa isn't real, I chose to ignore that information, took my place in line with Carol, and shuffled up the ramp for my turn with him. In our family, since only babies sit on parents' laps, I told Santa, "I'm too big to sit on your lap, I just wanted to meet you and tell you, you've been doing a good job!"

He beamed, and said, "Thank you, and Merry Christmas!"

"Merry Christmas," I replied, and walked down the back side of the ramp.

When we left Dayton's, dusk was enveloping the city and it was awash in streetlights and Christmas decorations. Mama said, "We'll go to a cafeteria for supper," and led us down the street. We picked up a tray at the end of the food bar and slid it past the wide array of choices, each priced individually. We chose meat loaf, mashed potatoes and gravy, and something called cole slaw, which looked exactly like the cabbage salad Mama made at home. Carol and I topped off our meal with a cookie, and Mama had a small piece of pie. After supper, she opened her purse and counted her money. "I have just enough left over to take us to a movie," she said.

The Radio City Theater was nearby so Carol and I skipped along as Mama led us to the box office and purchased our tickets under the blinking lights of the marquee. In our modest country attire, we walked through the genteel theater lobby, trying not to stare at uniformed employees, plush carpet, and soft lighting that seemed to be buried within the walls. Entering the darkened theater, we were greeted by a handsome usher in crisp uniform and jaunty hat. He beamed his flashlight along the floor, and we followed the circle of light to a row of empty chairs.

When we'd taken our places in soft velvet seats, Mama told us, "In this theater, they usually have a floor show before the movie begins. Tonight it will be 'The Inkspots.'"

"What are The Inkspots?" we asked her, picturing blobs of ink strewn about the stage floor. Before she could answer, four handsome black men strutted nattily onto the stage in front of the curtain. Dressed in white tuxedos with black pants and bow ties, they stood in front of the microphone, singing, gesturing and smiling in the bright circle of the spotlight. We had never seen a live performance other than the magician who performed before the annual Christmas movie at the Paramount Theater in St. Cloud. Fascinated, we absorbed their electrical energy, and let the harmony penetrate our souls and revive our tired but happy spirits. After their final bows, the curtains swept aside and the movie began.

When the movie was over, we had plenty of time to walk back to the depot. At mid-evening, the train station was quieter, so Carol and I explored. We spoke in hushed tones as our voices and footsteps echoed in the cavernous building, while Mama found a comfortable chair in the lounge, put her feet up and rested.

Soon, the monotonous voice of the caller announced the departure time of our train. Once underway, the clack of rails and muffled sounds of the train whistle lulled us into an exhausted sleep. Before we knew it, we were back in St. Cloud on the 10:40 p.m. train. Daddy was waiting for us when we got there.

The Gift

ಐೲ

It had been almost a year since any new toys had come into the house. The shiny pages of the Montgomery Ward catalog had long since been rumpled and tattered by the wistful little fingers of Santa's faithful, pinning their hopes on his bounty. Those of us to whom Santa was no longer real knew that Mama, in spite of her meager resources in these war years, would modestly provide one or two "perfect" gifts for each child in her large family. When we awoke on Christmas morning, we'd find the unwrapped presents in joyful array under the tree.

Our small house offered few places to hide parcels until Santa's visit on Christmas Eve. It was a long wait from year to year, and as the holiday neared, we children were often tempted to snoop through closets and shopping bags for a glimpse of what was to come.

One evening, about ten days before the holiday, we were home alone when ten-year-old Jerry mused with a glint in his eye, "I wonder where Mama hid the Christmas presents this year."

Wide eyed, we stare at each other in silence until Bernice finally voiced our thoughts, "Should we look for them?" Since our parents were away and the little ones asleep, conditions were ideal for a search.

"If they come home and catch us, we'll be in trouble!" Jean, the eldest and the one in charge, warned.

"Well, maybe we could just peek in a few places," Dick offered by way of compromise. We looked in Mama's closet and under her bed, but found nothing. The preliminary search had left our collective curiosity whetted and our consciences dulled. Now we were on a mission!

"Well, I guess we'll have to check out her special hiding place," Dick declared. He pulled up a wooden kitchen chair, climbed onto it and stood on tiptoe reaching for the ceiling. "I still can't reach," he said.

"Here," Dennis offered, brandishing the broom, "Use this! I tried it and know it works!" Dick grabbed the broom handle, shoved it against the trap door, lifted it slightly, and guided it aside revealing a two-foot square opening. A rush of cold air descended from its inky blackness

"We'll have to boost somebody up, somebody small," he said, then asked, "Who wants to go?"

"I do! Please let me, please!" I begged to be chosen for the important job, because it was my first year to be included in this grown up secret.

"Come on then," Dick said, "I'll boost you up." I climbed onto the chair beside him and stepped into his cupped hands. "Here you go," he said as I lunged through the opening and hung on with my elbows. One last push and I scrambled into the musty chamber pulling my skinny legs up after me.

Shivering from excitement as well as the cold air, I hunched on the floor joists letting my eyes adjust to the darkness, and for once, I was not afraid of the dark. The keen smell of home sawn lumber tweaked my nostrils from rafters so low I could barely stand upright in the center. "Remember to stay on the beams so you don't fall through the ceiling," Jean reminded me.

"I know," I answered, shoving some old picture frames and last summer's canning jars out of the way.

It was my job to grope through the darkness, feeling for the packages, then strike a kitchen match for light as I reported the contents to the waiting siblings below. One by one, I pulled items from shopping bags randomly tossed onto the joists. There was a hand made dress and coat for a doll, a red toy tractor, color books and crayons and a jump rope. I reached for the last item in a bag, and there I found the ball! The red and blue one with the stars around the center that Carol and I had seen in the dime store on our train trip to the twin cities. There were also things for my older sisters; perfume, a diary, hair ribbons, and pretty new socks. As I called out the contents to my audience below, they debated the likely recipient of each gift.

"You need to come down right now." As Jean reminded me, I happened upon one last package. It was a small glass globe on a little wooden stand. Inside were figures of a little girl, a Christmas tree, and a puppy. It was filled with liquid, and when inverted and turned upright, snowflakes gently swirled around the figures. It was the prettiest thing I'd ever seen! Forgetting about the cold, I kept turning it until the flame of the match I was holding touched my fingers. I lit another and played with the toy until that match burned out.

"What are you doing up there?" Jean worried, "Mama and Daddy will be home any minute! Reluctantly, I returned the globe to the shopping bag and crawled back to the shaft of light. Sliding on my belly over the opening, I dropped my feet into Dick's waiting hands, and he lowered me into the warmth below.

We pushed the trap door back in place and promised each other we wouldn't tell our parents of our misdeed. When we put ourselves to bed, I hardly dared to hope that the snowflake girl could be meant for me and fell asleep with snowflakes swirling in my dreams.

At last, Christmas morning came, but the globe was not under the tree. When my mother showed me the once magical gift, I could only imagine how she felt. "This was especially for you," she said, "But it got so cold in the attic that the water in the globe froze and burst the fragile glass."

Now, dull and lifeless, the snowflakes were gone and the figures bare and drab in the broken globe.

"Thank you, Mama." I reached for the broken pieces and tried in vain to recapture the vision of swirling snowflakes around a happy little girl, until finally I set it aside.

I wish I had told Mama that I saw it when it was beautiful, but I didn't. She never knew that for a few brief moments in that cold attic, her special gift had already made me happy.

Christmas Program 1942

ଓ୦ଓ

"Teacher" and her husband, Clarence, eat an early supper in the kitchen of their neat little bungalow in Sauk Rapids. She has just completed the final day of teaching before Christmas break. Childless, their quiet discussion centers on the evening plans. "You're sure you don't want to come with me?' she asks, knowing what the answer will be. He simply shakes his head, "no."

She hurriedly clears the evening dishes, and then sets out to drive the six miles over snowy, rutted roads to arrive early at the schoolhouse.

The first quarter moon, already risen, reflects off the snow and provides a faint glow as she walks up the broad concrete steps, takes a skeleton key from her purse and lets herself inside. She picks her way between the rows of desks in the darkened classroom and lights the two small kerosene lamps perched on brackets on opposite walls. The orange glow projects dimly. "Oh, dear," she clucks, "I hope someone brings an extra lantern or two so we can see the children as they say their lines."

She hangs her coat on the hook projecting from the wall behind her desk, slips off her wet overshoes and places them neatly underneath. Then, she puts her mittens back on and enters the dark, unheated coal room. Her thoughts on the evening ahead, she absently scoops a shovel-full of coal, brings it out and dumps it into the large heater that dominates the corner opposite her desk. She pushes the door shut quickly when a back draft of smoke billows the acrid smell of sulfur into the room. "And the bed sheets," she frets, "Will each family remember to bring one? We'll need them for stage curtains." Tonight, her twenty-eight students in grades one through eight will present the Christmas program. It is the most important social event of the school year and the only affair held in the evening at District Sixty School.

A sturdy, calm woman in her late thirties, Teacher is clad in her usual attire: a long-sleeved, hand-knit sweater, which she has just completed. She brought the project to school every day and, during recess, when the children were playing outside, she sat behind her desk and knitted on the sweater. Along with the sweater, she has pulled a grey, woolen skirt over tightly girdled hips and thighs. Warm, rayon hose and a new pair of flat brown, lace-up oxfords complete her ensemble.

Her long, dark hair, already flecked with grey, is woven into a thick braid at the nape of her neck, and she winds it around her head like a crown. Clear, grey eyes gaze from her big boned face, which is plain, but not unpretty, and devoid of makeup. She is known as a "sensible" woman, an expression that describes both her appearance and her philosophy of life.

These last three weeks have been busy ones for Teacher and for her students as well. With the taste of holiday sausage still on our tongues, our arrival at school on Monday after Thanksgiving found Teacher poring over her program manual, making plans for the pageant. We shook off our wraps, hung them in the cold entryway, and scurried to her desk, surrounding her with cold faces and sniffling red noses. What will she choose for each of us to perform?

After a hurried flag pledge and one verse of "America," Teacher meted out program assignments. On the big night, every student will recite a Christmas poem. The upper grade students will also perform plays and skits. Christmas carols sung by individuals, grade levels, or small groups will round out the program. By the end of the school day, we all had a copy of our "piece" to memorize at home.

The following days, we raced through reading, writing, and arithmetic classes to devote more time to practice. With her reputation as director at stake, Teacher prodded her charges into learning lines, speaking clearly, and singing on key. She met the challenges of this multi-age production with her customary patience and perseverance. Older students helped first-graders memorize four-line poems. Class clowns stood in the corner until they took the situation seriously. She was challenged by the occasional student born with a tin ear and singing hopelessly off-key. Shaking her head in despair, she moved me from group to group, admonishing, "Sing softly, Faye, softly."

It is finally program night! Suppers are eaten early, chores finished and children bundled for the ride to school. Cars and pickups enter the schoolyard, carving a trail through unplowed snow. Families tumble from cars, call greetings to one another and stamp snow on the unlit steps. A blast of cold air accompanies each opening of the door as they pour inside. The small room becomes crowded as parents squeeze into desks of older students or sit on long benches in the back of the room, holding babies and toddlers.

The conversations of men center around the latest snowfall, butchering and sausage making projects, chores, and the care of animals. The women discuss Christmas cookies and fruitcake, sewing projects; and home remedies for sick children. "Mary Lou had such a bad cough, so I made a hot mustard plaster and put it on her chest," one declares.

"But, you must be careful so it doesn't burn her tender skin," another interjects.

"I still find the best remedy is to let them breathe the steam from the teakettle," still another offers. Sniffles and coughs can be heard around the room, as if to emphasize the women's concerns.

The children are decked out in their best Christmas apparel for this important occasion. For the girls, a new dress made from fabric Mother has been saving or cut from a castoff garment. No one wants to wear a flowered feedsack dress for this occasion. The everyday long brown stockings that Carol and I usually wear are replaced by smooth white ones. There are ribbons and curls in our hair instead of the usual pigtails.

Before bedtime last night, Mama wound each of her daughter's hair in curlers. She unraveled the braids, and then dipped a comb into a glass of water and starting at the top of the head, made a part straight down to the ear. She soaked the first section in water, clamped a tin curler on it and rolled it like a sausage alongside her daughter's face. She repeated the procedure at one-inch intervals until eight or ten curlers, four inches long, stood like tin soldiers surrounding our heads. The curlers poked our scalps and we tried to sleep on our faces; but we endured the discomfort in hopes of having ringlets like Shirley Temple, as well as our more fortunate curly-haired cousins. In the morning, when she took the curlers out, Mama wound the tresses around her fingers to make long curls. The curls soon fall straight in Carol's and my resistant hair, and the night of torture with the curlers is of little avail.

The boys, too, look their best. Sporting fresh haircuts that were given by Mother in her lamp-lit kitchen an evening or two ago, and slicked down with water or tonic. They are wearing their church clothes; their best freshly ironed shirts and trousers, and a necktie, too, if they happen to own one.

A couple of thoughtful families bring gasoline lanterns; one is set on Teacher's desk, giving a bright white glow, and another on the washstand in the back of the room. Enough bed sheets have been accumulated to make curtains for the stage. To hang them, Uncle Ed and his son, Eddie, string a wire across the front of the room. The sheets are flung over the line and secured with safety pins. Most of the sheets are an assortment of flour and feed sacks, sewn together and hemmed. Some still bear traces of Nutrena feed labels or the Occident flour logo. Between acts, when the curtains are closed, the audience reads, "Good baking is no accident with Occident." Along with my classmates, my skin prickles with anticipation as we wait for final preparations to be completed. We place our gifts under the sparse branches of the pine tree, which we have proudly trimmed. In our minds, we can still feel the dry paste that clung to our fingertips when we made endless chains from red and green construction paper. Giddy with the excitement of having all the parents present, we sense a bond with our school friends as we share our small desk with another to conserve space. We whisper and giggle while we wait for the program to begin, knowing Teacher is at a safe distance behind the curtain, where she gives last minute instructions to the older students in her calm, quiet voice.

The program is finally underway. The children are introduced, and each strides to the front of the room to recite. After practicing nightly with their children, parents strain to catch the words as their child, overcome by timidity, mumbles into her collar. Teacher is aware of the shyness that prevails in children living in a community with few social contacts outside of their families. While one child might revel in the special attention, another might burst into tears of fright, seeking refuge in her mother's lap.

Half-way through the evening, it's Dick's turn to declaim the lengthy poem, "Jest 'Fore Christmas," by Eugene Field. In it, he relates all the mischievous activities he loves. He finally tells us:

> Most all the time, the whole year 'round,
> There ain't no flies on me,
> But, jest 'fore Christmas,
> I'm good as I can be!

He has been practicing the long lines, which are so descriptive of him, until I, too, have memorized them and could prompt him if his memory failed.

Then Carol and I are called to recite, "The Night before Christmas." unaccustomed to the spotlight, we shy little sisters walk up together and stand very close, arms touching. It would be inconceivable for one of us to recite the long poem without the support of the other. Night after night, we've practiced until we know the words by heart. We take a deep breath and plunge into the long narrative. Our confidence grows and our voices become steady as the words tumble out in singsong fashion. When one of us falters, the other maintains the pace until we wish a Happy Christmas to all and to all a good night!

Teacher deftly maneuvers her charges through each performance, guiding and prompting. She knows which students she can depend upon to know their lines and which ones haven't practiced at home and need prompting. The recitations are interspersed with songs or a playful skit, until each student has appeared onstage two or three times. When it is my turn to sing with a group, Teacher again reminds me, "Sing softly, Faye, softly!" In my exuberance, I sing "Joy to the World!" loudly and joyfully, and as off-key as ever!

The program ends with the traditional nativity scene. A boy and girl in the coveted roles of Mary and Joseph contemplate the savior in the form of a doll that lies in an apple box filled with straw. Shepherds and wise men bow, heads covered with bath towels kept in place by elastic bands. Angels in long dresses hastily constructed from more feed sacks, and with tinsel in their hair, complete the scene. Strains of Silent Night float through the winter night, and the program is over!

There is a loud banging on the door and it flies open! "Santa!" shriek the students in delight, while toddlers whimper and cling to parents. Bells a-jingle, and with a merry "Ho ho," Santa strides to the front of the room, a gunnysack filled with candy and peanuts over his shoulder. He drops his bag by the Christmas tree and demands, "Have you been good?" in a voice vaguely familiar. Then, Santa calls the names for the gift exchange. With a scarcity of toys in the large families, each child wants their gift under the tree to be a toy from Woolworth's or Kresge's dime store: a rubber ball, a slate, a ring, or a yo-yo.

Wrappings litter the floor as twenty-eight children open their small gifts; a few disappointed because a parent spent the required ten cents on pencils, tablets, or erasers. Santa also gives every child in the room a bag of candy and peanuts. Then, waving goodbye, he disappears amid a jingling of bells.

The din of excited children mixes with the crunch of peanut shells being stepped on as they fall to the floor amid the wrappings. Candy is sampled and savored on little tongues; ribbons of colored sugar folded into "s"-shapes and hardened. The spicy cinnamon taste of red stripes and the peppermint taste of candy canes mingle with the salty crunch of peanuts.

There are gifts for Teacher, too. Each family struggles to bring something. It might be a dozen eggs gathered earlier in the day from the hen house; or some carefully chosen homemade Christmas cookies, shaped like bells, stars or angels. Other popular gifts are a freshly butchered chicken, or some homemade pork sausage. The children eagerly gather around teacher's desk and bask in her kindly gratitude, as one by one, she accepts the practical gifts.

When it is time for leave-taking, a lantern is hung in the entry where children don coats and caps, then scramble through piles on the floor to find overshoes and mittens. Parents bundle drowsy toddlers and herd their families into the cold December night. This night has been a special one for the children, and when it is over, they are reluctant to see it end. Snow is falling, and they open their mouths to catch the flakes, and then close their eyes to feel it gently fall on their lashes.

One by one, frigid vehicles, dozing in a half circle on the driveway, come to life. Their lights illuminate the frosty air and pierce the exhaust that swirls around departing families. Final season's greetings are called, car doors slam, and the chain of lights snake out the driveway and down the road.

Alone in the deserted building, Teacher closes the door to the outside draft and tries to rub away the ache in her shoulders as she surveys the empty room. Then, resolutely, she begins to pick up gift-wrappings. She slides the desks back in rows, sweeps up peanut shells, and takes down and folds the stage curtains. She'll let the fire burn out in the stove, as heat won't be needed in the schoolroom for the next two weeks. Finally, she gathers her gifts, blows out the flames in the wall lamps, and walks out through the darkness to her waiting car.

Explosion!

෨෦෬

The small kerosene lamp that stood in the middle of the linoleum-covered kitchen table was adequate to illuminate our table at mealtime, but left the rest of the room in shadows. In the long winter darkness, most of the family's activities had to center around that lamp on the kitchen table.

One evening after work, Daddy stopped at Ladner Hardware Store in St. Cloud, and bought a Coleman gasoline lantern for Christmas. The new lantern gave off a brilliant glow that illuminated the entire kitchen, soon replacing the kerosene lamp on the middle of the table. It used white gasoline, and air was pumped into the gas tank to keep the flame bright. When the flame grew dim, one pumped it up, much like hand pumping a bike tire.

It was about nine o'clock on a bitterly cold New Year's Eve, when the gas lantern played a near tragic role in the life of one of our family members.

The little ones had already been put to bed for the night, and some of us were listening to the battery-powered radio in the corner of the kitchen. Mama and Daddy were busy at the kitchen table, cutting up the last of a hog they had butchered earlier. Fourteen-year-old Bernice added a few sticks of kindling to the fire in the kitchen stove. Then, she replaced the stove lid, filled the teakettle, and set it over the flames for hot water to shampoo her hair. At age fourteen, my older sister Bernice was slim and tall. She had sparkling brown eyes and beautiful dark brown hair. She was one of those people who didn't have to grow up to become attractive, but had been pretty all her life. Bernice took good care of her appearance and was always perfectly groomed in spite of our not having indoor plumbing and a bathroom. She was brushing her hair by the kitchen sink when she noticed the light in the lantern growing dim.

"Pump it up, will you, Bernice?" Mama requested, her hands busy wrapping meat.

As Bernice pushed down on the pump, there was a sudden "Poof!" as gasoline squirted out, spraying her upper body! When the gasoline squirted, she instinctively brought her arm to her face, covering her eyes. In the same split second, she was engulfed in flames from her waist up, the fire devouring the gasoline on her skin and clothing.

In an attempt to escape the flames, her first reaction was to run toward the outside door. Daddy stopped Bernice before she reached the door, then grabbed a winter coat that hung on a hook beside the door, and wrapped it around his burning daughter. He patted it against her arms, her face, and her hair, until all the flames were smothered. His quick thinking saved Bernice's life, and minimized scarring as well, because he was able to extinguish the flames so quickly.

When the fire was out, we could see the extent of Bernice's injuries. The outer layer of skin hung loosely on her face and neck, and the fire had penetrated her cotton dress, burning her skin underneath. Both of her hands were also burned, but the deepest burns were on the arm she had raised to protect her eyes.

It all happened in a few short seconds, but the picture of our sister in flames was imprinted indelibly on our minds. We stood frozen in fright as Mama grabbed a quilt from her bed and wrapped it around Bernice, while Daddy rushed into the frigid night to start the car. They must get Bernice to the hospital immediately! We had no telephone to call the doctor or to alert the hospital.

On the way to the St. Cloud hospital, Bernice, sitting alone in the back seat, said she prayed all the way, stopping only to comfort her crying mother in the front seat. Still in shock, Bernice consoled, "Don't cry, Mom, it doesn't hurt," then continued to pray aloud.

When Daddy asked her what she was saying, Mama interjected, "I don't think she knows what she's saying, she's delirious."

Years later, in relating the story, Bernice said she wanted to tell Mama, "Yes, I do know what I'm saying!" However, in those days, children would never presume to correct a parent, so Bernice remained silent.

With no phone at home, we children waited and worried, until our parents returned from the hospital and told us of Bernice's condition. They got home very late, but we were still awake, anxious to hear what they had to say. We were relieved when Mama assured us that Bernice was going to be all right.

"When the doctor arrived," she said, "He advised the nurses not to peel the loose skin away, so they swathed Bernice's burns in balm, wrapped her deepest wounds, and gave her something for pain. She was resting comfortably when we left." We felt safe now that our parents were back at home, and we knew Bernice would get better. We all went back to bed, and fell into an exhausted sleep. When we awoke in the morning, it was New Year's day, the beginning of a new year, and a day to thank God for sparing our sister's life.

At the hospital, it was near midnight when Mama and Daddy left Bernice and came home. She was still awake when she heard the church bells at St. Mary's Cathedral chime twelve times. When the medication began to take effect, she finally dropped off to sleep to the sounds of nurses wishing each other a Happy New Year. It was the beginning of a long, painful stay at the hospital for Bernice.

During her stay in the hospital, Bernice was under sixteen years of age, and was therefore placed in a special children's ward where she could receive no visitors except her parents. Grandpa Carlin, a widower well into his seventies, lived at St. Benedict's on the south side of St. Cloud. No longer driving, and unfamiliar with the rule, he trudged across the entire city to visit his granddaughter in the hospital. When he got there, he was told that the hospital policy was strictly enforced, and that he wouldn't be allowed to see Bernice. Tired and disappointed, the old man pulled his cap back down over his ears, buttoned his overcoat tightly around his neck, and began the long, icy trek back across town.

Monica Misho, one of the teachers from Sauk Rapids Jr. High School, where Bernice was a student, also came up to the hospital to see her. The elderly single woman, one of many who continued to teach well into old age, because of poor teacher retirement benefits during that era, took a nickel of her hard-earned money and, out of the kindness of her heart, bought a candy bar for Bernice.

Bernice remained in the hospital for more than three weeks. It was a happy day when she could finally come home, but she would spend another two weeks recuperating before she could go back to school. Her burns healed well, and left few permanent scars, none on her beautiful face and neck. The deep burns on her arm left a scar, which she still carries, more than sixty years later.

Goodnight, Grandpa!

֍

Grandpa lived on the same farm for over fifty years. It was located in a grove of evergreens about a half mile from ours, on a narrow sandy road that branched off at the pond just past the schoolhouse.

At seven years old, I had never sat on his lap, chatted with him or held his hand. I don't think he ever talked to me or looked directly at me. I was curious about him, in awe, and somewhat frightened of him, so I contented myself with watching him from what I felt was a safe distance, as though I could see him but he couldn't see me. When it came to his numerous grandchildren, Grandpa showed no partiality. He seemed to be indifferent to all of us.

Now, Grandpa was past eighty, and the years had taken their toll. His life had not been without its sorrows. He buried his wife in 1927, and before that, three infants, including twins; and a grown son as well. He had seven remaining adult children, four daughters and three sons. My father was his youngest son.

He was not a very big man but had tremendously big patches at the knees of his bib overalls that seemed to cover most of his legs. I could see the buttons of his long underwear at the neck of his shirt all year around. The shirt was a faded blue chambray in the summer, which he rolled halfway to the elbows exposing the long sleeves of his underwear. In winter, it was a plaid flannel shirt, navy blue and red, buttoned tightly around his neck and sleeves on coldest days.

His forehead was broad and his receding hair was white and wispy. Bushy white eyebrows almost obscured his black deep-set eyes and a thick white mustache, which offset his prominent chin, gave him an intense look making him seem austere and remote.

Summers on the farm, he wore a big straw hat brought down from the attic each spring and ringed with the sweat of decades of stacking hay and oats in the hot summer sun, and plowing and cultivating crops behind a team of horses from dawn until dusk. When he removed it at mealtime and for church on Sunday his scalp was pink under his wispy snow-white hair.

Mostly, I remember him in his dress clothes. He still cut a dapper figure in his one black suit with a crisply ironed white shirt and dark tie, which he wore to church every Sunday, even on the hottest of days. At summer family gatherings, after church he would leave the tie, hat and suit coat in his square Model A Ford, his narrow black suspenders a sharp contrast to his white shirt.

His joints were stiff with arthritis and the knuckles oh his hands bony as he sat on his straight-backed wooden kitchen

Jacob Bromenschenkel, 1940.

chair. Born in 1863 of German immigrant parents he understood English but preferred to speak in his native German. He spoke very little as the conversation flowed about him, but when he did quietly join in, his was still the final word.

His children, grown though they were, still anxiously tried to impress and please him, deferring to his opinions and seeking his approval. When he sat at the table, his adult daughters waited on him and fawned over him, helping him to fix his plate and giving him the best cuts of meat. They chattered and tried to make conversation with him. His reaction was one of impatience or gruff tolerance.

He wouldn't have been Grandpa without the wine colored felt bedroom slipper he always wore on his left foot. In later years, he suffered from a foot injury that developed into gangrene and resulted in the removal of the big toe. It

didn't heal properly, causing him to lean heavily on a cane as he shuffled to get around. In spite of his disability, he went out every day to tend the chickens and do what he could around the farm. Once wiry and muscular and still a strong man, he groused because he could no longer shock grain, husk corn, milk cows or tend livestock.

Jacob Bromenschenkel and Mary Klaesges, wedding day, November 19, 1889.

I wondered, What does a foot look like with the big toe missing? How does it feel to have a toe cut off? I tried to imagine my own small foot without a big toe. We small cousins were curious, but it would have been unthinkable to ask grandpa to show us the foot with the missing toe, so we respectfully kept our distance.

"It's going to rain," I overheard Grandpa tell Daddy one day, "My foot always lets me know when it's going to rain," Without the benefit of radio or television for weather forecasts, I was impressed with Grandpa's special power. How could a missing toe cause you to predict the weather?

Grandpa's son and daughter-in-law Hank and Teen and their only child, 7 year old Agnes lived with him and did most of the farm work. I saw Grandpa often when I came to their house to play with my lively and noisy cousin, but he never spoke to me on my visits and I never expected he would. His stern countenance did little to invite familiarity and I was shy around him.

One winter evening, I stayed overnight at their house after walking the half-mile home from the country school with Agnes. It was bitterly cold after supper, so Uncle Hank told Agnes and me to stay inside with Grandpa while he and Teen did the chores. It would take them at least two hours. We were disappointed because we loved to be in the barn at chore time to play with the calves and feed oats to the horses.

Besides, I was uneasy about staying inside with Grandpa. A shiver crawled up my spine as I stood by the kitchen window and watched them head down the hill to the barn. The glow of their lanterns grew dimmer until it was finally swallowed by the closing of the barn door.

When I turned around, the house felt empty and quiet compared to the noisy din of all my brothers and sisters in our own small home. I could hear the ticking of the clock and the crackling of the embers in the kitchen stove as Grandpa sat at the homemade kitchen table in the glow of the lamp-light and read The Farmer paper. He spoke not a word to us as we joined him at the table, his only sound the rustle of the paper as he turned the pages. When he finished reading The Farmer, Agnes and I noisily worked the puzzles in the children's section while he paged through the St. Cloud Daily Times. Eventually, he picked up his ancient black prayer book and used a magnifying glass to read the tiny German print. Then, wordlessly, he scraped back his chair, rose and shuffled quietly into his cold bedroom.

On such a cold night, it was chilly inside the big farmhouse, even though the heater in the front room had been banked with coal and fire was aglow in the wood burning cook stove. To warm up, and perhaps because Grandpa wasn't there to tell us to be quiet, Agnes and I played a rousing game of hide and seek. With so many places to hide, it was a favorite game. In the soft light of the kerosene lamp on the kitchen table, it was easy to find shadowy recesses in the pantry, washroom, stairway and dining room.

We must have been playing very loudly because suddenly Grandpa was standing in the kitchen in his long woolen underwear. I was afraid, and thought he was going to scold us for awakening him. He shuffled across the expansive kitchen to the lantern that hung by the basement door, struck a match, raised the globe and lit it. Then he said quietly and kindly, "I'll put you to bed." He led the way, cane in one hand and lantern in the other. He leaned his cane against the wall and grasped the banister as he slowly ascended the steps. Agnes and I obediently followed.

In her room at the head of the stairs, we quickly undressed down to our long underwear while Grandpa slid open the heat register on the floor to warm the room from the heater below. We jumped into the icy bed while Grandpa fumbled with the quilts and tucked them around our ears. He patted us gently and said, "Say your prayers," and without another word picked up his lantern; shuffled out the door and down the hallway. We called, "Good night, Grandpa!" as the light receded. If he answered, we didn't hear him.

Grandpa died on December 28, 1949 at the age of eighty-six when I was thirteen years old. Outside of that incident, I don't remember ever having a conversation with him.

The Boxcar

80)CG

We could hear the gears grinding and the roar of the powerful engine even before we could see the truck coming. My brothers and sisters and I ran to the edge of the yard and watched in awe as the big truck slowly pulled its heavy burden down the gravel road. When it reached our farm, the driver got out, surveyed our narrow rocky driveway, then removed his cap and scratched his head. "This'll be a challenge," he told Daddy, shaking his head. "The driveway is awfully narrow, and there's a four-foot drop on each side. It'll be tough to make the turn, pulling this forty-foot rig."

The boxcar was finally here! We had all been waiting for it since early morning. Soon, our family would no longer be crowded into our two-room house. The boxcar would provide the space needed for the children's bedrooms.

Daddy sent us all inside, and Mama said we had to stay there, so we'd be out of the way, as the driver maneuvered his cumbersome load across the driveway and through the yard.

We crowded around the small windows in our house, and craned our necks to see the activity. There was much backing up and pulling forward as the driver struggled to position the boxcar in just the right spot along the back of our small house. It had to be positioned exactly right, because once he unhitched it from his tractor, there'd be no moving the boxcar. When he pulled it within two feet of the house, Daddy was satisfied, so the driver unhooked the stabilizing bars, put blocks under it where the wheels had been, and drove away.

When he was gone, we flocked out of the house, ran around to the back and inspected our newest property. It was forty feet long and eight feet wide, and jutted out six feet on each side of the original house, so if one stood by the barn and looked westward, the house was "T shaped.

When Daddy slid the heavy door open, we clambered inside the cleanly swept railroad car, all talking at once. "Where will our room be?" Carol and I pestered Mama. The plan was to put two double beds into one of the bedrooms, then Jean, Bernice, Carol, Mary Ann, and I would all share the same room.

"We'll divide it into three rooms," Mama said. "The girls will sleep on the north end, the boys on the south, and we'll have a little room in the middle where we'll put a nice warm stove."

"Daddy will cut a hole in the wall," she added. "So we can get here from the rest of the house."

The boxcar was painted a brick red. On the side was a four-foot high, white logo with the words, "Great Northern" stamped in a circle. Inside the circle was an illustration of a mountain goat, standing on his hind legs, his forefeet resting on a mountaintop. High up on each end, next to the roof, was a small removable door, its opening used as a chute to fill the boxcar with grain and other staples before making its journey across the flatlands of the Dakotas and the mountains of Montana, on its way to Seattle and back. There were narrow ladders leading to the high end doors, which my brothers immediately climbed. "Get down," Mama commanded, then said, "Daddy will remove those ladders so no one gets hurt."

While we explored and played around the building, Mama and Daddy made plans for converting it into a dwelling. Windows had to be cut, doors installed, and then the inside finished out to make it habitable. "It's a good thing we have all that lumber in the back yard," Daddy said.

Employees of the Great Northern car shops in Waite

Park were allowed to strip the outdated boxcars and keep the lumber, so Daddy spent long evenings dismantling old box-cars no longer in use. In the meantime, lumber piles steadily grew in our back yard, competing for space with the old farm equipment he no longer used.

They would line the walls and ceiling with this boxcar lumber, and cover the floors with six-inch square, red clay tiles. Then, Mama would paint the bedrooms; the boys' room blue, and a sunny yellow for the girls. Finally, they would cover the outside of the boxcar with siding that came in a roll and resembled imitation brick.

Today, in the empty railroad car, Mama remarked, "We certainly have our work cut out for us, don't we?" Daddy did-n't seem to be listening. He was already measuring the walls to cut holes for the windows.

First Communion

෨◌ඏ

It was a clear, sunny day in May when Dennis and I received the sacraments of Penance and Holy Communion for the first time, at St. Augustine's little basement church in East St. Cloud when we were in the second grade.

The church decreed that, at age seven, we had reached the age of reason and were ready to participate in this great mystery of the Catholic Church. We could now be taught the meaning of words like consecration, examination of conscience, contrition, penance, and the most impressive of all, transubstantiation.

Cousin Agnes, Faye, Jackie Thering, Hilde Prom, Shirley Stark, brother Dennis.

To explain the consecration, Father Louis, our aged priest, led us into the first two pews of the empty church, and stepped behind the altar. His voice echoed in the quietude, as he held up a thin, round wafer and a chalice containing a few drops of wine. "These will still look the same," he told the twenty-five bewildered second-graders. "But they will actually become the body and blood of Jesus during the consecration of the mass. This is called 'Transubstantiation.' You must remember that word." He then asked, "Is it clear to you?"

We nodded our heads solemnly and answered, "Yes," but wondered at this great mystery of transformation, this eating of another's body and drinking his blood. Although we didn't completely understand, we trusted in God completely and believed in his ability to do anything, so we accepted it without question. We didn't realize, as we sat in the quiet, shadowy church that day that the lessons we'd be learning at age seven would be the foundation of a faith that would last a lifetime.

There were many prayers to learn before we could receive these sacraments. We practiced them at home for weeks, and again at catechism class on Saturday mornings. The Our Father, Hail Mary and prayer to our Guardian Angel were familiar and came easily to us, but we struggled with the historic tenets of faith in the long and confusing Apostles Creed. Also, as seven-year-olds, we found the Act of Contrition to be a wordy and cumbersome way of apologizing to Jesus. We didn't feel like sinful children, and detesting our sins was a foreign concept to us, but Sister told us it simply meant being sorry in our hearts when we do something wrong.

We had Catechism class every Saturday morning. Since Daddy worked on Saturdays, our uncle Ed would stop at our driveway and take us with him. Even though his car was already filled, he would good-naturedly tell us to pile in on top of his family for the five miles to church, and then drop us off again on the way home. "Thanks for the ride!" we'd holler when we jumped out and slammed the door. The next Saturday, as regular as clockwork, he would be waiting at the end of our driveway, again.

We had many good nuns who taught our Saturday morning catechism classes, but my favorite was Sr. Marold. She was a slim, beautiful woman who wore her flowing black veil like a crown. When she spoke, her voice was sweet, warm and lovely. When she sang, I thought it must have been what Angels sounded like. She told us that God loves children, and loves our prayers. It made them easier to learn, and once we did, we were proud to offer them to God. We all felt loved by Sr. Marold, and she said it came from God.

Sister told us that in order to receive Jesus in Communion, our souls must be free of sin. By confessing our sins to a priest in the sacrament of penance, they would be forgiven. Then, our souls would be white and clean, ready to receive Jesus. We weren't sure just where our soul was in our body (most of us thought it was in our wrist) but we all knew we wanted it to be white and clean.

"I will teach you five things necessary to make a good confession," Sister said. She gave each of us a sheet of paper and instructed us to draw around our hand. "For each finger, you will have one thing to remember about confession," she said, then listed them:

Think of your sins. Be sorry for them. Tell them to the priest. Say your penance. Promise not to sin again.

The first step, thinking of our sins, required much time and thought. One must have a decent, presentable list with not too many sins, but not too few either. Then, there was the question of what would qualify as a sin. Was it a sin to forget to pray? And what about extenuating circum-stances? Was it a sin to hit your brother if he broke your crayons, or hit you first? Since children didn't sit with parents in church, but occupied the front pews, the forbidden whis-pering and giggling with one's friends during mass was surely a sin that we could use. Once we came up with a basic list of sins we were comfortable with, we felt it was simpler just to stick with the old standbys in subsequent confessions.

A few days before Communion Sunday, an afternoon practice was mandated. We would review our catechism, and then practice the ceremonial protocol for the special mass. Our parents enlisted the help of Teacher, who would drop my brother, me, and four cousins off at the church on her way home from school. Since practice extended over the supper hour, our parents gave us a few cents to stop at Carl's Grocery for a snack.

Teacher, a non-Catholic, suggested we pool our money and buy a few wieners instead of candy. "Would you like to come home with me?" she invited. "You can eat them at my house, and then I'll take you back to church. It was a special treat for us to visit Teacher's neat little bungalow, and eat at her tiny kitchen table.

Later, we excitedly told our parents about our unexpected visit to Teacher's house, and the hot dog supper. We weren't prepared for their reaction. "Today is Friday!" Mama scolded. "We don't eat meat on Fridays!" Although Teacher apologized and insisted she hadn't remembered the Friday ban, our mothers all remained suspicious. Teacher's good deed went unthanked; and we children were all instructed to remember that sin in our first confession the next morning.

After catechism class on Saturday, Father Louis entered the confessional, placed a stole over his shoulders and waited as one by one, the penitents entered. He sat in a small, dark, windowless room, barely large enough for his chair. On either side of him, a curtain covered a sliding opening, behind which the penitent knelt in his own tiny room.

When it was my turn to enter the confessional, it took all the courage I could muster to propel my small legs to the closet-sized room. I slipped inside where the only light was that which filtered through the curtain hanging over the doorway. There was a built-in kneeling bench, and it creaked softly as I knelt on it, and then rested my folded hands on the ledge beneath the screened opening. I could feel my heart beating as I went over my memorized list of sins. When my turn came, I would tick them off on my fingers and get it over with as soon as possible.

There were indistinct whisperings between Father and the penitent on his other side, then the sliding sound when he closed that door. In a second, the door on my side slid open. I took a deep breath and whispered into the curtain, "Bless me Father, for I have sinned. . ."

After Father heard my sins and assigned a penance, I made an Act of Contrition. The weeks of practice put me in good stead, and I recited the memorized prayer without hesitation. Then, Father gave me absolution and I was free to go back to my pew and say the Hail Mary he gave me for a penance. Now, I was ready to receive First Communion.

Our First Communion took place on a bright, sunny morning in May. We had to be very careful to stay away from the kitchen and the water pail, because it was strictly forbidden to eat or drink anything after midnight before receiving Communion. I had a new, white dress and long, white stockings, held up by round elastic garters just above my knees. My brown hair, wound in tin curlers instead of pigtails the night before, was crowned with a gauzy veil. Dennis wore a white shirt and tie, as well as white trousers. Mama and Daddy gave us a new prayer book and a small rosary that we would take to church each Sunday for many years. Dennis received a black prayer book and mine was white. On the cover of my book, covered in clear celluloid, was a picture of the Blessed Virgin Mary, wearing a blue mantel, and gazing serenely from under a golden crown, as queen of Heaven and earth.

We arrived at St. Augustine's early, and lined up with a partner just as we had practiced. We waited for the organ to begin playing, and then with hands folded, we processed down the center aisle and took our places, girls on one side, boys on the other. During mass, we answered the catechism questions we had studied all year, and then renewed our baptismal vows. Finally, it was time to receive Communion, when Jesus would become a part of us. Minutes later, the mass was over and we gathered outside the church, visiting with neighbors and taking pictures before we headed home. There were four families of my cousins who made our first communion on the same day.

After church, Mama made a big chicken dinner. Dennis and I played outside with our siblings, and we were given first privileges at jump rope and the rubber ball for bouncing and playing catch, because it was our special day. We had no living grandmothers, but our grandfathers came for dinner, as well as Godparents and some uncles, aunts and cousins. The grownups kept telling us, "This is the happiest day of your life!" and we were very happy.

At dinnertime, there wasn't room for everyone around the table, so our siblings had to wait until the first ones were through eating and the table was reset. Since it was our special day, Dennis and I got to eat with the grownups when all the best pieces of chicken were still on the platter when it was passed around the table. Of course, we both asked for a drumstick.

Buster Brown Shoes

ଋଚ

On Saturdays, the house had to be cleaned, floors scrubbed, and shoes polished for church on Sunday. Most Saturdays, a couple of chickens had to be butchered, then, cakes, pies or donuts made. It was a busy morning for Mama and all of her daughters.

Also, every Saturday morning, Smilin' Ed McConnell hosted the Buster Brown show on the radio. During the program, I hoped I wouldn't be called on to carry in a pail of water or an armful of wood, because I didn't want to miss a minute of the heroic tales of boy wonder, Buster Brown and his famous dog, Tige. They had exciting adventures on trains and ships, in caves and haunted houses, in the mountains and at the seashore, with Buster Brown always wearing his wonderful namesake shoes. Tige barked and the music swelled, as time after time, the boy with the famous shoes saved the day. Every few minutes, Smilin' Ed reminded children everywhere to ask their parents for Buster Brown shoes so they might have similar adventures. Then, he invited them to join him in singing this little ditty:

> You got shoes
> I got shoes
> Everybody's gotta have shoes
> There's only one
> kind of shoes to have—
> Good old Buster Brown shoes!

In my off-key voice, I wholeheartedly joined the chorus. Each Saturday morning, the magical adventures became my own, and of course, I was always wearing a pair of mystical Buster Brown shoes in my dreams.

One day, Mama said, "School will be starting soon, and it's your turn to get new shoes, Faye."

After going barefoot all summer, it was exciting to think I might get my Buster Brown shoes at last. *Now I'll get them!* I thought, *I'll finally have my adventure shoes!* Carol and I went shopping with Mama. We went to the shoe department in J.C. Penney's and sat down in a row of chairs fastened together. A shoe salesman perched in front of us on a little stool with a slanted front. I put my right foot on the slant, clad in last year's scruffy shoe, its broken shoelace tied in a knot.

"We need to measure your foot, but first, I need to untie this shoe," he announced with a grimace.

"Here, let me." I said and expertly picked the knot and kicked off the shoe. He measured my foot and left for the storage room. When he came back, he was carrying three cardboard boxes. One by one, as he removed the covers and folded back the paper, the smell of new leather gently wafted forth. I breathed it in, its fragrant aroma adding to the excitement of receiving new shoes. The shoe clerk pulled out the first shoe and slipped it on my foot.

"Stand up," he commanded, pinching the tip of the shoe and squeezing the instep each time I tried one on. "Where does your toe come?"

"About there," I answered, pointing vaguely to the tip of the shoe and thinking, *My toes can't see, so I don't know how far they come.* Finally, we had a good fit.

"These must be Buster Brown shoes! They are, aren't they? I asked, hopefully.

"No-o," the clerk replied, "They aren't."

"O-h-h!" I said, wondering if the wrong kind of shoes would break the spell.

He looked at Mama and her children in their home-made dresses, and said, "Buster Brown shoes would be a bit more expensive". Then, after a pause, "Would you like to see a pair?"

Please say yes! I thought as I crossed my fingers, but dared not look up. It seemed like a long time before Mama answered.

"Wel-l, we could look at a pair," she replied, glancing at me. The clerk returned with a pair of shiny black shoes, made of soft, smooth leather and slipped one on my foot. He pinched the toe again, and squeezed the sides. It fit perfectly! "We'll take them," Mama said with a smile, then turned to me, "Would you like to wear them home?" I nodded vigorously as the clerk slipped the left shoe onto my foot and tied it snugly. My feet seemed to float as I wore the shoes out of the store.

Outside, Mama fumbled in the bottom of her purse and found a few nickels and pennies. "Here, girls," she said, "Take this and get some ice cream." Eyes a-light, Carol and I glanced at each other in anticipation. We held out our hands and Mama counted a nickel and five pennies into each. "Hold it tight so you don't lose it," she reminded us, "I have a little more shopping to do so I'll meet you in a few minutes. She walked back into J.C. Penney's and we headed down Main Street to the ice cream parlor three doors away.

Enroute, we pondered our choices. We could order two scoops of vanilla, which we call "White," chocolate, or strawberry ice cream. We've been here before, and know the treat will be served in a long stemmed clear glass dish; and we'll use a slender, silver spoon that reaches all the way to the bottom, so we won't miss a taste.

There were no customers in the shop as we walked importantly across the black and white tile floor to the soda fountain that stretched along the wall, and then hiked our-selves up onto a tall stool. Although shy, and on our best grownup behavior, we couldn't resist the urge to twirl completely around on the red leather perch, then swivel it back and forth, our skinny legs dangling midway to the floor. Every now and then, I stole a glance at my brand new shoes. The fountain clerk walked over and leaned his elbows on the counter, his friendly face smiling. "Hello ladies, what will you have today?" he asked. We giggled self-consciously at being called ladies, and then asked him politely what kind of ice cream he had, stalling for time in making our decision.

Finally, I told him, "I'll have white." Carol ordered chocolate. We watched his scoop as it glided across the surface of the ice cream and rolled it into a smooth ball, and then we loosened the grip on our money. Already the coins were so warm and moist that a penny or two stuck to the palm of our hands as the rest tumbled out on the counter. We seldom have "store-bought" ice cream, and in our minds, we were already tasting its cool, creamy softness. In our family, we made our own ice cream.

Usually, on the way home from St. Augustine's church on hot Sunday mornings, Daddy stopped at the East Side ice-house. For a quarter, the ice man clamped a sixteen inch square block of ice in his tongs, pulled it out of its sawdust home, and plopped its icy wetness onto the floor in the back seat of the car, amid a tangle of children's legs. When we got home, the ice tumbled into the galvanized laundry/bath tub that usually hung on the back of the house. Dick and Jerry each grabbed a handle and carried the cold burden into the shade.

While Daddy stayed in the car and read the Sunday paper, the boys chopped the block into small pieces with an ice pick and Mama stirred milk, cream, eggs, sugar and vanilla together and poured it into the six-quart ice cream can with the dasher inside. She set the can into the wooden freezer bucket and packed salt and ice in layers around it. Finally, she connected the crank to the top of the dasher, and the children took turns rotating it. The ice cream stiffened in the can from the icy water around it, and the colder it became, the more difficult it was to crank. When it became too stiff to turn, Mama came out and pulled the dasher out, re-covered the container and packed more ice around it so it would continue to harden. The children all helped to make it, and all looked forward to eating its delicious coolness for dessert after Sunday dinner.

Today, we have "boughten" ice cream, a rare treat that we've tasted only a few times in our lives. We dipped the small roundness of the spoon into the dish and savored it slowly, each taking a tiny taste of the other's flavor. Finally, the long spoon reached the bottom, so we tipped the dish to our mouths and slurped the last melting drops. By the time we finished, Mama was back.

"Was it good?" she asked.

"M-m-m-m, it was delicious!" we agreed, smacking our lips.

On the way out of the ice cream store, I asked Mama, "Do you think this is an adventure?"

"Yes," Mama smiled, "I think it is."

Happily, I reached for the shoebox containing my worn-out shoes, hooked my fingers into the string that the clerk tied around it, and swinging it, followed Mama and Carol out the door. Already, I was imagining all the other adventures I'd have in my brand new Buster Brown shoes!

Agnes

My cousin, Agnes, and I were babies at the same time. When I was five and a half years old, my parents built a farmstead about a half mile from the home place where Agnes lived with her parents and our grandfather. Thus began five years of friendship and adventure on the farm between Agnes who was an only child, and me, sandwiched in the middle of twelve children.

Her cousins were all born into large families, but like us, she, too, had few toys during those post depression and World War II years. Also like us, the farmstead was her playground and she wholeheartedly embraced it. At chore time, her mother worked alongside her father, milking cows, feeding stock and cleaning barns. Either Agnes would be free to tag after them with animals as her companions, or she would be left to her own resources. In this environment, she grew as strong, sturdy and self reliant as any little farm boy.

Visiting Agnes at her farm was exciting in more ways than one. Grandpa had spent a lifetime building up the place and everything was bigger and better with far more places to play and hide than our small farm. Besides, if anything or anywhere was off limits to Agnes, it presented a challenge she couldn't resist. I loved walking the half mile down the dusty road to her farm, and enjoying all the freedoms we didn't have at home.

Every summer in August, the oats fields were cut, and the grain bundled and stacked into shocks to dry. On threshing day, the bundles were thrown into the thresher where the oats was separated from the stems. The oats flowed into a wagon to be stored in the granary. The stems or "straw" were blown onto a pile behind the barn for later use as bedding for the animals. To us children, the straw stack was a glowing mountain, glistening in the sun, seeming almost as high as the barn. A perfect place to climb, then sit on its slippery surface and slide down, but our parents didn't see it that way.

Children weren't allowed to climb the straw stack because if there were holes in it, the straw got wet and moldy when it rained. Moldy straw couldn't be used to keep the cows and calves dry in their pens. All farmers were strict about that. Agnes repeatedly assured me as I looked longingly at their giant straw pile, "Honest, we don't have that rule here," so we gleefully climbed up and slid down. As a precaution though, we played on the back side where we wouldn't be spotted by adults.

We loved playing in their dairy barn. It was built into the side of a hill with a drive-in hay mow and oats bin on the ground level. The lower level snugly housed the milk cows, young stock, and horses. Our favorite spot was the hay mow where we'd swing on the rope slings used to stack the hay up

Calves on Grandpa Jacob's farm, 1940.

to the rafters. While Agnes's parents were milking the cows beneath us, we'd scramble to the top of the hay, grab the rope, and whooping and hollering, zoom across the length of the barn like acrobats in a circus. We'd start at opposite ends of the barn and sometimes collide in mid-air. Miraculously unhurt, we dropped like rag dolls onto the driveway of the hay mow. "What's going on up there?" one of the adults would yell.

"Nothing," we'd yell back. Catching our breath, we'd keep on swinging.

I was afraid of the work horses. I felt dwarfed by their huge clopping hooves, wide rumps, and shaking heads as they whinnied and snorted when Grandpa unharnessed them after a day in the fields. Only when they were secure in their stalls did I approach them. The oats bin was directly above their manger with a sliding door in the floor where Agnes and I pushed the oats down into their trough. "Fill it half full and no more," Hank insisted, but we pushed the slippery grain down until the box overflowed into the hay manger and around the horses' feet. It was an extra job for her busy parents to scoop some oats out so the horses wouldn't overeat, but they didn't scold us for things like that.

The barn was also home to a bull, kept in a sturdy pen. The powerful animal was tethered to a post by a chain connected to a ring through his nose. His only freedom, periodic trips to the cow yard to breed the cattle. We children were instructed to stay away from his pen. If we came near, he lowered his immense head and ominously pawed the ground, so we had no trouble taking another route to the calf pens.

Sometimes, when no one was in the barn, Agnes would invite us into the pen to ride the calves, something else we couldn't do at home because of risk of injury to the young calf's back. Once, when we were about seven years old, Agnes assured me again that they didn't have that rule, and I was more than eager to believe her. We were having a wonderful time. One of us drove the calves to the manger where

124

the other was perched ready to jump onto a calf's back, only to slide off as the skittish steer kicked up its heels and bounded away. "Try a smaller calf," we yelled at each other, "They're easier to stay on!" Engrossed in our dastardly deed, we didn't see Agnes's mother come down the barn steps brandishing a switch she had cut from a willow tree.

She yelled at us, "Get off those calves!" Without using the switch, she made an impression on us. Now and then, we still rode the bigger calves, but only when we knew her parents were both working in the fields.

One Summer Sunday, when the grownups were visiting at Grandpa's house, several cousins were playing outside. Agnes asked us if we'd ever been to the top of their silo. "No! Have you?" I asked her.

"Sure," she said, "You can see ever so far from up there! Let's do it now. Come on up, I dare you!" No one had ever told us we could not do that, we reasoned, so one by one, a half dozen of us climbed the steel rungs on the chute inside the silo. When we reached the top, we pulled ourselves up onto the roof. There was a little rope barrier about two feet high along the edge of the roof and we hung onto that, feeling proud of our bravery.

As we were looking across the pasture, our mothers appeared in the cow yard below. They must have been panic-stricken but called to us quite calmly, "Come down, right now!" They didn't punish us, but after our descent, each mother warned her offspring," There will be dire consequences if you ever climb to such heights again!'

I was always envious of Agnes's beautiful brown hair. It was long, thick and curly while mine was thin, wispy and straight with a scrawny pigtail behind each ear. On special occasions, after shampooing her hair, Agnes's mother would wind it around her fingers into long "Shirley Temple" curls that were so popular in the early '40s. Most of the time, though, her mother parted her hair in the middle and braided it into French braids. Starting with three strands, she braided, adding more hair as she went along. Each time she added another strand, the little girl howled louder. "Ow! Ow!" she yelled.

"Hold still!" her mother yelled in reply. It was the only time I was glad I didn't have her hair. Later, whenever I asked Agnes if it really hurt, she would never tell me. The braids looked so pretty on her, too. Not even those tight braids could straighten that curly hair. All the little short hairs curled around her braids like a curly halo around her head.

At Grandpa's house, a battery operated radio sat on a little table in the corner of the kitchen. We had no radio at our home, and were fascinated by the prospect of unseen voices coming from the magic box. We loved listening to it. Agnes, an only child, was used to the radio, and more interesting in playing when we came to visit. One day, when Aunt Teen was outside working, I wanted to listen to the radio and Agnes wanted to play. It was a standoff, with neither of us ready to give in, when Agnes played her trump card. "I just remembered," she said. "Mama said we can't have the radio on because we'll wear the battery down. Then, I'll get a scolding." One didn't argue with a mandate from a parent, so I reluctantly turned the radio off, and we went upstairs to play in her room.

Agnes had her own bedroom at the top of the stairs. There were three other empty, unheated bedrooms up there, and after sleeping three in a bed in our own crowded house, I couldn't imagine what it would be like to have my own bed and my own room. She had a few toys in her room, including a child's table and chairs and a set of tin doll dishes. When it wasn't too cold, we would play house in her room. For refreshments, she would borrow from her mother's baking supplies on the pantry shelf. Her favorites were white raisins and currants. She'd take her little teapot and fill it half full of water. When her mother was outside working, she'd find the brandy bottle on the shelf, add a few drops to the teapot and serve it. Once, when five- year-old Carol was playing with us, she took a sip of the brandy water and coughed. "Oh, oh," six-year-old Agnes said, "You're too young, you can't have any more," so she and I drank the brandy water.

In the summer, Agnes was supposed to herd the cows in an unfenced field. Her parents invited me to keep her company. We needed to keep them away from the haystacks and out of the nearby sprouting cornfield. To break the monotony, we took Agnes's beautiful, thick storybook out to the meadow and I read the stories aloud. We leaned against the haystack reading, and neglected to watch the cattle. They wandered away and ate from the stacks. Sometimes they got into the cornfields, and Hank and Teen would have to help us bring them back. Hank would sit down, take us by the arm and patiently explain how it wouldn't do to let the cattle trample the corn. We felt bad, agreed with him and promised to try harder, but the same thing would happen again the next day. Finally, Hank decided the cattle were no match for our storybook, and our cow herding days were over.

Hank and Teen liked to go to Mass very early on Sunday mornings. They loved their little girl and if she asked them, they'd sometimes stop and take Carol and me with them to St. Mary's Cathedral instead of our tiny basement St. Augustine's church in east St. Cloud. It was exciting to walk up all the big steps and through the massive wooden doors of the church. Inside, somber voices singing and responding in Latin echoed from the high ceilings as we took our seats in a pew next to a huge granite column. As the Mass droned on, Agnes would whisper in her mother's ear, and then turn to us. "Come on," she'd say, "We're going to the bathroom." She, Carol and I would find the bathroom, a treat compared to our cold outhouses at home. We'd use it and flush it a few times, and then the three of us would sneak up the winding staircase to explore the no-longer used choir loft. We would look down and survey all the people praying, as well as the priest, far away at the altar, offering Mass with his back to us. Now and then, a toddler spied us and we would wave or stick out our tongue and giggle. Then Agnes, unfettered by the shyness that plagued Carol and me would crawl among the pews playing hide and seek. She would pantomime and whisper loudly to us. Carol and I were afraid an adult might discover us so we stood to the side and didn't join in, but we enjoyed the respite from the long Mass. The next time we went to Mass at St. Mary's, the bathroom idea was Carol's and mine.

When we were almost 10 years old, our beloved uncle Hank was killed in a car accident. His family, which now consisted of his widow and two children, sold the farm and moved into St. Cloud. My farm adventures with Agnes were over and we began to grow in different directions, but never far from the memory of the fun and mischief we shared over sixty years ago.

The Afternoon Off

ള🙊

School was in session a month, and I thought about how different it was riding the bus into town. There seemed to be so many changes in my life those days. *It isn't that I want to go back to the old school*, I thought, *It's just that I wish I would fit in better at this one; that I wasn't so different.*

Life was so simple last year in the little white schoolhouse a few steps down the road from our home. It was practically filled with brothers, sisters, and cousins whom we knew so well. Classes were different, too. The one teacher for eight grades was like a mother hen, clucking among her charges: prodding, scolding, and cajoling. It was acceptable to raise one's hand and join in the discussion of whichever class happened to be in session; a comfortable place to be.

It was 1948, and last year was the first that school busses were sent to rural areas to pick up high school students. This fall, they will also take seventh and eighth graders. Last year, there were only three people in our seventh grade class: my cousins Hilde, Clarence, and me. In the fall, we'd join an eighth grade class of twenty-two strangers. Hilde and I sat on the steps of the school we had attended since first grade and shared our apprehension about changing schools.

Mainly, we were concerned about the town kids who would be our new classmates. Were they really lazy, spoiled, and stuck up, as we had been told? And would they call us "dumb farmers" as they sometimes did our older siblings? After a lengthy discussion, and since we didn't know any town kids, we decided to reserve judgement. "We'll just have to wait and see what it's like," we agreed. "It'll be different, that's for sure."

On the first day of school, I waited at the end of the driveway with my siblings Bernice and Jerry. My feelings were a mixture of trepidation and curiosity as the sun glinted on the noisy yellow bus coming down the road. Thirteen-year-old Jerry, who was already a sophomore, assured me, "It won't be so bad."

The engine roared, the driver clutched, and with grinding gears, grated to a stop on the loose gravel. We entered and barely started down the aisle when the door clicked shut and the crowded bus careened forward. The final passengers on the route, we lurched off balance and hung onto seats as we searched for a vacant one. I felt embarrassed when boys remarked, "Ooh, who are you? Jerry, you didn't tell us you had a cute little sister!" No boy had ever said that about me before, and I didn't know how to respond. At eleven years old, I wasn't interested in boys and thought their remarks were crude. Just then, a strange girl moved aside and patted the seat. I gratefully accepted and rode to school in silence.

The eighth grade classroom was on the second floor of the Russell school building as Hilde and I followed others into the room, found a desk and sat down. Everyone seemed to know each other, and most already looked like teenagers as they buzzed excitedly from group to group.

The teacher walked in, a short dour woman in her early sixties. Her short arms hung limp at the sides of her thick body, and her legs were the only part that moved as she slowly crossed the front of the room. Her brown, finger-waved hair was parted on the side and secured in a narrow roll along the nape of her neck. She peered over silver-rimmed glasses, and her unsmiling face dropped in several layers from chin to neck to ample bosom. Scowling at the class, she told us to sit down and be quiet, then related the rules. When she read the class list, she used the students' legal names, and from then on, I was expected to answer to the strange name of Frances. She pronounced it "Frawncez."

As the weeks went by, school settled into a routine and there were some things that I really liked about it. Friday was current events and library day. Each student had a weekly newspaper that told us about strange places around the globe. One week we studied about Iran and saw pictures of natives planting their fields with oxen. Miss Perlowski told us the country is pronounced, Ee-ron! And the library! I still couldn't believe we had a whole room devoted to books! In district sixty, we had a little cabinet of books, all of which I'd read by the time I was in fourth grade.

One of my favorite things about this school was that every Tuesday afternoon, the ninth grade girls glee club sang in the room across the hall. Their voices floated through the transom, sounding like a concert. The music caressed my ears, and sometimes I closed my eyes and imagined the girls on a blue stage, wearing white gowns and singing "Toora, Loora, Loora," an Irish lullaby.

The eighth grade girls were tiresome, though. Most of them stood in little groups and talked about their hair, tugging on their clothes over budding curves, and whispered about boys they liked. They filled out their perky white blouses with the artificial flowers pinned at the collar while my slender, eighty pound body was as straight as a board, my clothes hanging limply from bony shoulders. They were older and more sophisticated; for the first time in my life, I noticed a difference between my age and that of my classmates.

That year, other issues came to my attention for the first time, too. Having a big family in those post-depression years meant that money was used only for necessities, and I became aware of the differences that living a frugal lifestyle made in a young person's life. It meant not having money in your pocket to walk to the drugstore with classmates for a soda or shake. It meant wearing blue jeans and tee-shirts, when other girls had pretty new clothes.

There were also social differences I hadn't noticed before. Many of the students had different lifestyles than mine. They were privy to advantages that I was not, advantages that I longed to have. Some classmates played the piano or a band instrument, and some took dance lessons. They were able to stay after school for extra-curricular activities, and most seemed to have more social confidence than I had. I thought if I could be more like them, maybe I'd like school better.

I need an afternoon off! I mused. *I need to do some things that town girls get to do; a little exploring, maybe spend some time in town with a friend. Who would be willing to do this with me? Hilde, of course. We do everything together.*

I'd been thinking about it for some time and trying to get the nerve to ask Hilde. We both heard of people skipping school, but neither of us knew anyone who had actually done it. Hilde may not go along with it, but on the other hand, I thought she might be ready for some time off, too. Finally, I popped the question. "Hilde," I said. "Let's take the afternoon off!"

"What?" she said. "That's skipping school! You're crazy! We can't do that. What if we get caught?" Finally she asked, "When?" and I knew I had an accomplice.

"How does tomorrow sound?" I asked.

"I don't think I can do that," she said regretfully. But we continued to imagine what we'd do if we had the afternoon off, and how we'd pull it off if we decided to go ahead with the plan.

"We could write excuses for each other," I suggested, then added, "We'll make the final decision tomorrow." A year older than me, I was hoping she wouldn't decide to be the responsible one and back out.

The next morning on the bus, Hilde asked, "Do you think we could really get away with it?"

"Of course," I answered. "Nobody will ever know."

I tore a sheet from my notebook and wrote, "Please excuse Hilde to help at home" and signed her mother's name. She did the same for me. The rest of the way to school, oblivious to the noisy din, we practiced writing like our mothers. Many erasures and smudges later, we arrived at Russell Junior High, excuses in hand.

It was a long morning. The big brass pendulum on the wall clock swung rhythmically in time to its "tick . . . tick . . . tick." We unfolded, refined, and refolded our notes time and again before the noon bell rang. To avoid suspicion, Hilde gave Miss Kennedy, the principal (better known as T.K.) her excuse after English class at eleven o'clock. I bravely handed mine over during the lunch rush at noon. T.K. glanced at it, glared over rimless glasses and snapped, "Are you sure?" I nodded, intently picking at a fingernail, and T.K. muttered something about this being on the up and up, before disappearing into her office.

We were free! I flew down the two flights of stairs and outside where Hilde was waiting with our bag lunches. We skipped down the street, leapfrogging over fire hydrants and savoring the sweet, fresh taste of freedom. We planned to eat our lunch under the shady oaks in the park along the riverbank, but decided to explore under the Mississippi bridge. Nibbling on sandwiches, we perched on huge, flat boulders that jutted out of the water, all the while sharing our secrets. The pebbles we threw made ripples in the diamond studded water, and bread crumbs sailed away instantly on the swift current. Skipping nimbly from rock to rock, we laughed at each other's knock-knock jokes and felt proud to have fooled T.K.

Suddenly, shrieks hung in the air as I lost my footing! I gasped at the water's chill as it swirled around my legs, while clawing for a hold on the smooth boulders. Hilde grabbed my arm and hung on as I struggled to gain a foothold on the algae covered stones. In a moment, which seemed like forever, I scrambled onto the safety of a flat rock.

"You idiot!" Hilde shouted. "Why can't you be more careful? You are so clumsy!" I emptied the water from my shoes and wrung out my socks. Shivering with fright, we looked at each other, then I began to giggle. Hilde soon joined in and we sat on the rock, laughing hysterically as huge tears of relief rolled down our cheeks.

I spread my socks in the sun, and announced, "Let's go shopping." Neither of us had ever been shopping without our mothers, and the nearest shopping district was in St. Cloud, more than two miles away. We reviewed the route in our minds: from the drugstore, past the Spotlight Cafe, across the tracks, past the fairgrounds as far as Benny's Lunch on St. Germain Street. Turn right, cross the Mississippi bridge, and we're practically downtown.

My feet squished in wet shoes and socks as we began our journey. More jokes. More secrets. "I don't like boys, do you?" I asked.

"No," Hilde answered. "Well . . . Jon is cute."

"But he's so stuck-up," I pointed out. "I like Robert better."

"Boys only talk to popular girls," Hilde lamented.

"Who cares?" I insisted.

"Step on a crack, break your mother's back," she chanted, changing the subject. We walked in silence, concentrating on cracks in the sidewalk. After the first mile, the sun persuaded us to cross to the shady side of the street.

The fairgrounds marked the half-way point. Bare and deserted, it was hard to imagine a tent city existed here just a few weeks ago.

"Did I ever tell you what did at the fair one time?" I asked Hilde.

"Nope, what?"

"Not much. I lost most of my money. It was in a tent, you know, where they have little steam shovels. You put in a dime and try to pick something up."

"Oh, no!" Hilde groaned.

"Well, there was this statue of a girl; she was wearing a pink dress and she had a puppy, a cocker spaniel, I think. Anyway, it was beautiful, and I really wanted it. Every time I picked it up with the steam shovel, time ran out before I got it to the edge, so I kept putting in another dime until I ran out of money."

"Did you ever get the statue?"

"Nope."

"You should know better than that!" Hilde lectured. "I'd never waste my money like that. It was your own fault. What did your ma say?"

"I didn't tell her, but she'd have said the same thing."

We crossed the Mississippi and passed the Hays theater where we looked at scenes from a Ma and Pa Kettle movie. "Our family saw this movie," I told Hilde. "We really liked it, maybe because we finally found some folks poorer than we are!"

Hilde laughed, "Us, too."

The scant repertoire of movies we'd seen included a few titles such as *Little Women, The Yearling,* and *Lassie Come Home.* Having brothers, we saw more Westerns than anything, but in junior high, girls don't admit to liking Gene Autry and Roy Rogers, the singing cowboys.

We finally reached Seventh Avenue. It was cool in the Five and Dime Stores where we browsed and planned to buy a Coke with the dime Hilde had in her pocket. Crossing the street, our eyes caught the clock on the big yellow dome of the courthouse. It was already 2:15 P.M. We had an hour to walk to the two and a half miles back to school before the bus left. We'd be in big trouble if we weren't on it when it stopped at our driveway.

We quickly spent Hilde's dime at the soda fountain in Woolworth's.

"I'm so thirsty I could drink this all myself," Hilde said, between gulps. I held my breath. "But . . . I'll share," she added and reluctantly pushed the small glass my way.

"Thanks," I breathed, and drained the glass, slurping the ice cubes.

One by one, we re-passed familiar landmarks. We were hot and hungry, and our feet ached from the hard concrete. We had long since abandoned joke telling, and our old adversary, conscience, was beginning to bother us.

"Maybe we shouldn't have done this. What if we get caught? It was your idea, you know," Hilde worried.

"If we get to the bus on time, I think we'll be okay." I tried to reassure both of us, limping from a blister on my heel. Neither of us had a watch, and we quickened our pace as the Indian summer sun sneered at us

Back at the drugstore corner, we could see the busses lined up in front of the school. We ran the last two blocks up the hill and, out of breath, clambered aboard. Grateful for the security of the bus, we enjoyed the cool air that blew through the open windows as we began our meandering route home.

The next morning on the bus, we discussed our escapade. "Do you think anyone will find out?" Hilde asked.

"Nah," I replied. "Don't worry, we're safe."

Back in the classroom, the boys shot spitballs at the girls, punched and shoved each other. The girls gathered in groups and giggled. In English class, students took turns reading monotonous stanzas of *Ivanhoe* aloud, while their peers stared out the window dreaming of baseball and movie stars. Later, we worked the dreaded story problems in math. "If Farmer Jones has eighteen rows of pumpkins, how many wheelbarrows will he harvest if he doesn't get an early frost . . .?"

Yesterday was already fading from our memories when we heard a soft tap on the classroom door. The knob turned and the door opened quietly. Looking up, my eyes locked with a pair of black, steely ones squinting through rimless glasses. A slight smirk on her face, T.K. slowly raised her right hand and beckoned with her forefinger.

She called Hilde first. She seemed to have been gone a long time, and when she came back didn't glance at me, but stared at the floor. The only sound in the room was the "tick . . . tick . . . tick . . ." of the clock, then I heard, "Frances," as T.K. beckoned once more. I carefully slid my pencil into the slot at the top of my desk, closed my math book, got up, and followed T.K. into her office.

A Goodbye

So many things changed within me during my first year in town school, by spring nothing seemed the same. The magic of childhood was stealing away, and the stir of adolescence brought with it shyness and introspection. That which I thought was silly in my classmates was now happening to me, as I, too, began to notice my clothes, my hair, and boys.

By spring, I discovered many feelings that confused me, especially in dealing with the boys. I had my first crush on Robert, and he on me. He had dark brown, curly hair and a friendly smile. I thought he was the cutest boy I had ever seen in my life. We shyly exchanged school pictures and hoped to catch a glimpse of each other in the hallways between classes. One day, I wore a new yellow dress to school. A day or two later, I found a note in my desk. I read, "Dear Frances, I wanted to tell you this for a long time. I love you. You look so pretty in your yellow dress. Love, Robert." I told myself that it was silly, squashed it and threw it in the wastebasket. Immediately, I regretted it, but my pride wouldn't let me retrieve it.

Always independent and tomboyish, I felt that I should be relating to Robert a little differently than my six brothers, but I didn't know how to go about it. On the last day of school, at our picnic in the park, the boys brought their bikes and would give the girls rides. "Want a ride, Frances? Robert asked shyly.

"No, thanks," I answered independently. "I'm perfectly capable of walking." He quickly rode away, and I wondered why I answered him so curtly as I watched him give someone else a ride.

We had been away from the country school for a year when Hilde and I went back for a visit. How everything had changed. The school room looked so small and crowded. How noisy it seemed with all the little children scampering about. We felt older and out of place in that environment, and relieved to no longer be there.

Later that afternoon, I needed to be alone, so I took a walk through the fields along the pasture fence to the tree line. I sat in their shade and tried to sort out things in my mind. The birds were singing and a breeze was sighing through the trees as I gazed across the meadow that I loved. At twelve years old, I was no longer a child and didn't belong to that world any longer. In September, I'd be a freshman in high school and on my way to growing up. I wondered if I would be ready to meet the challenges of those new and exciting years.

What would the future have in store for me? That question was impossible to answer, but I was already learning something very important: Life is an unfolding mystery, full of changes, and each change can be an adventure!